QA
37.2
U45
1990

UMAP

Modules
Tools for Teaching 1990

UNIVERSITY OF ARKANSAS AT MONTICELLO
RECEIVED
OCT 22 1991
LIBRARY

published by

Consortium for Mathematics and
Its Applications, Inc.
60 Lowell Street
Arlington, MA 02174–4181

edited by

Paul J. Campbell
Beloit College
Campus Box 194
700 College Street
Beloit, WI 53511
campbell@beloit.edu

All rights reserved. No part of this publication may be reproduced, stored in a retrieval system, or transmitted in any form or by any means, electronic, mechanical, photocopying, recording, or otherwise, without prior permission of the copyright holder.

Recommendations expressed are those of the authors and do not necessarily reflect the views of the copyright holder.

© 1991 COMAP, Inc. All rights reserved.
ISBN 0–912843–19–5
Printed in USA.

Table of Contents

iv

Introduction

The instructional modules in this volume were developed by the Undergraduate Mathematics and Its Applications (UMAP) Project. UMAP has been funded by grants from the National Science Foundation to Education Development Center, Inc. (February 1976–February 1983) and to the Consortium for Mathematics and Its Applications (COMAP), Inc. (February 1983–February 1985). Project UMAP develops and disseminates instructional modules and expository monographs in the mathematical sciences and their applications for undergraduate students and instructors.

UMAP Modules are self-contained (except for stated prerequisites), lesson-length, instructional units from which undergraduate students learn professional applications of mathematics and statistics to such fields as biomathematics, economics, American politics, numerical methods, computer science, earth science, social sciences, and psychology. The modules are written and reviewed by classroom instructors in colleges and high schools throughout the United States and abroad. In addition, a number of people from industry are involved in the development of instructional modules.

In addition to the annual collection of UMAP Modules, COMAP also distributes individual UMAP instructional modules, *The UMAP Journal*, and the UMAP expository monograph series. Thousands of instructors and students have shared their reactions to the use of these instructional methods in the classroom. Comments and suggestions for changes are incorporated as part of the development and improvement of materials.

The substance and momentum of the UMAP Project comes from the thousands of individuals involved in the development and use of UMAP's instructional materials. In order to capture this momentum and succeed beyond the period of federal funding, we established COMAP as a nonprofit organization. COMAP is committed to the improvement of mathematics education, to the continuation of the development and dissemination of instructional materials, and to fostering and enlarging the network of people involved in the development and use of materials. COMAP deals with science and mathematics education in secondary schools, teacher training, continuing education, and industrial and government training programs.

Incorporated in 1980, COMAP is governed by a Board of Trustees:

David Roselle, President	University of Delaware
Robert M. Thrall, Treasurer	Rice University, Retired
William F. Lucas, Clerk	Claremont Graduate School
Linda M. Chaput	W.H. Freeman & Co.
Margaret B. Cozzens	National Science Foundation
H. Newton Garber	Garber Associates, Inc.
Landy Godbold	The Westminster Schools
Marion T. Jones	Devitt-Jones Productions, Ltd.
Trudi C. Miller	Univ. of Minnesota–Minneapolis
Jewell Plummer–Cobb	Cal. State Univ.–Fullerton
Henry Pollak	Bell Comm. Research, Retired

Instructional programs are guided by the Consortium Council, whose members are elected by the broad COMAP membership, or appointed by cooperating organizations (Mathematical Association of America, Society for Industrial and Applied Mathematics, National Council of Teachers of Mathematics, American Mathematical Association of Two-Year Colleges, The Institute of Management Sciences, and American Statistical Association). The 1991 Consortium Council is chaired by Margaret Barry Cozzens (National Science Foundation), and its members are:

Ronald Barnes	University of Houston–Downtown
Donna Beers	Simmons College
Richard G. Brown	Phillips Exeter Academy
Alphonse Buccino	University of Georgia–Athens
Paul J. Campbell	Beloit College
Toni Carroll	Siena Heights College
Margaret B. Cozzens	National Science Foundation
Gary Froelich	Bismarck High School
Bernard Fusaro	Salisbury State University
Frank R. Giordano	U.S. Military Academy
Landy Godbold	The Westminster Schools
Charles Hamberg	Illinois Math & Science Acad.
John Kenelly	Clemson University
Peter Lindstrom	North Lake College
Kay Merseth	Univ. of California–Riverside
Walter Meyer	Adelphi University
Fred S. Roberts	Rutgers University
Stephen Rodi	Austin Community College
Gene Woolsey	Colorado School of Mines

This collection of modules represents the spirit and ability of scores of volunteer authors, reviewers, and field-testers (both instructors and students). The modules also present various fields of applications as well as different levels of mathematics. COMAP is very interested in receiving information on the use of modules in various settings. We invite you to contact us.

UMAP

Modules in
Undergraduate
Mathematics
and its
Applications

Published in
cooperation with
the Society for
Industrial and
Applied
Mathematics, the
Mathematical
Association of
America, the
National Council of
Teachers of
Mathematics, the
American
Mathematical
Association of Two-
Year Colleges, The
Institute of
Management
Sciences, and the
American Statistical
Association.

Module 699

Mortality Discount

Ho Kuen Ng

**Applications of Mathematics of
Finance to Actuarial Science**

COMAP, Inc. 60 Lowell Street, Arlington, MA (617) 641-2600

INTERMODULAR DESCRIPTION SHEET:	UMAP UNIT 699
TITLE:	Mortality Discount
AUTHOR:	Ho Kuen Ng Department of Mathematics and Computer Science San Jose State University San Jose, CA 95192
MATHEMATICAL FIELD:	Mathematics of finance
APPLICATION FIELD:	Actuarial science
TARGET AUDIENCE:	Students in courses on finite mathematics or probability
ABSTRACT:	This unit introduces the basic theory of life contingencies.
PREREQUISITES:	Acquaintance with the basic concepts of compound interest and probability
RELATED UNITS:	Unit 681: Simple Mortality Functions, by H. K. Ng

© Copyright 1989 by COMAP, Inc. All rights reserved.

Mortality Discount

Ho Kuen Ng
Department of Mathematics and Computer Science
San Jose State University
San Jose, CA 95192

Table of Contents

MODULES AND MONOGRAPHS IN UNDERGRADUATE
MATHEMATICS AND ITS APPLICATIONS (UMAP) PROJECT

The goal of UMAP is to develop, through a community of users and developers, a system of instructional modules in undergraduate mathematics and its applications to be used to supplement existing courses and from which complete courses may eventually be built.

The Project was guided by a National Advisory Board of mathematicians, scientists, and educators. UMAP was funded by a grant from the National Science Foundation and is now supported by the Consortium for Mathematics and Its Applications (COMAP), Inc., a non-profit corporation engaged in research and development in mathematics education.

COMAP Staff

Paul J. Campbell	Editor
Solomon Garfunkel	Executive Director, COMAP
Laurie W. Aragon	Development Director
Philip A. McGaw	Production Manager
Roland Cheyney	Project Manager
Laurie M. Holbrook	Copy Editor
Robin Altomonte	Administrative Asst./Distribution
Dale Horn	Design Assistant

1. Introduction

Most of us are familiar with interest discount. Roughly speaking, the discount factor v is today's worth, or present value, of an amount of money which will grow to one unit after one year. Assuming an interest rate of i per year, we can easily derive that $v = 1/(1 + i)$. Readers can refer to any elementary book on finance for this fact. A good source for review is [Kellison 1970].

Let us now add uncertainty into our consideration. What is the present value of one unit that is payable after one year only with a probability of p? Mathematically, let Y be a random variable representing a payment after one year, with

$$Y = \begin{cases} 1 & \text{with probability } p \\ 0 & \text{with probability } 1 - p. \end{cases}$$

Letting $PV(Y)$ denote the present value of Y, we are interested in calculating $E[PV(Y)]$, the expected value of the present value of Y. Using elementary statistics, $E[PV(Y)] = 1 \cdot v \cdot p + 0 \cdot v \cdot (1 - p) = vp$. Although we should call it the *expected present value* to be really accurate, people usually just call it the present value.

Let $_np$ denote the probability that a payment will be made n years from now. Thus $1 - {}_np$ is the probability that such a payment will not be made. If the amount of the payment is A, then its present value is $A \cdot v^n \cdot {}_np + 0 \cdot v^n \cdot (1 - {}_np) = A \cdot v^n \cdot {}_np$.

2. Mortality Discount

One of the most important applications of the study of contingent payments is in the calculation of insurance and annuity premiums. Let us first introduce some notation. We use (x) to denote a person currently at age x. For such a person (x), we let $_np_x$ denote the probability that (x) will survive at least n years, and $_nq_x$ the probability that (x) will die within n years. Of course the sum of these two probabilities is equal to 1. The probability $_np_x$ is sometimes called a *mortality discount* if the contingency is survival, because, as we will see in the next few sections, it can be used in exactly the same way as the factor v^n in discounting future payments to the present time. To distinguish between these two, we call v^n the *interest discount factor*, and $_np_x$ the *mortality discount factor*. The following sections will illustrate how these two factors can be used to calculate the present value of future contingent payments.

"...We calculate the present value of future contingent payments."

1

Exercises

In all the exercises, unless otherwise stated, we assume that for $0 \leq x < 100$,

$$_np_x = \begin{cases} (100 - n - x)/(100 - x) & \text{for } 0 \leq n \leq 100 - x \\ 0 & \text{otherwise,} \end{cases}$$

and that the interest rate is 7%. The above mortality assumption is known as de Moivre's Law. See [Ng 1987] for other simple mortality assumptions.

1. What is the probability that a 20-year-old will die before reaching age 60?

2. What is the probability that a 20-year-old will die between ages 70 and 80?

3. Pure Endowment

A *pure endowment* to (x) after n years is an amount payable at the end of n years to a person currently at age x if (x) is alive; no payment will be made if (x) dies within n years. If the amount of the payment is A, the pure endowment can be represented by the random variable Y, where

$$Y = \begin{cases} A & \text{with probability } _np_x \\ 0 & \text{with probability } _nq_x. \end{cases}$$

Then the present value of this pure endowment, i.e. $E[PV(Y)]$, is $A \cdot v^n \cdot _np_x + 0 \cdot v^n \cdot _nq_x = A \cdot v^n \cdot _np_x$.

We can see that to calculate the present value is to multiply the future contingent payment A by two factors, v^n and $_np_x$. The first factor accounts for interest, because money today can accumulate interest to a future time. The second factor accounts for mortality, because there is a chance that the payment will not be payable in the future due to death. These are the reasons why they are called the interest discount factor and the mortality discount factor respectively, as mentioned in **Section 2**.

Exercises

3. What is the present value of a pure endowment of $100 after 10 years to a person currently at age 40?

4. Mr. X wants to set up a college fund for his son who is now 10 years old. He figures that if his son reaches age 18, he will need

$40,000 for his college education. If he dies before reaching 18, of course he does not need anything for college education. Mr. Y is willing to furnish this college fund if Mr. X gives him its fair value now. What should Mr. X give to Mr. Y?

4. Life Annuity

A *whole life annuity* is a promise to pay a certain amount at the end of each year for as long as a person, known as the annuitant, is alive. (To be more precise, this is known as an *annuity-immediate*, the payments of which are made at the end of each period. An annuity with payments at the beginning of each period is known as an *annuity-due*. In this article, we only consider the first type of annuity.) Suppose this annual amount is A and the person's age is x. We note that the probability that (x) will survive n years and then die in the next year is $_n p_x \cdot _1 q_{x+n}$. With this probability, the person will receive n annual payments with total present value $Av + Av^2 + \cdots + Av^n$. Summing over all possible n, we have the (expected) present value

$$\sum_{n=1}^{\infty} \left(Av + Av^2 + \cdots + Av^n \right) \cdot _n p_x \cdot _1 q_{x+n}$$

$$= A \sum_{n=1}^{\infty} \sum_{m=1}^{n} v^m \cdot _n p_x \cdot _1 q_{x+n}$$

$$= A \sum_{m=1}^{\infty} v^m \sum_{n=m}^{\infty} _n p_x \cdot _1 q_{x+n}$$

$$= A \sum_{m=1}^{\infty} v^m$$

$\cdot$ (the probability that (x) will survive at least m years)

$$= A \sum_{m=1}^{\infty} v^m \cdot _m p_x .$$

Let us try to interpret the above sum using interest and mortality discounts. We can view the whole life annuity as an infinite sequence of pure endowments, or an infinite sequence of contingent payments, say, $P_1, P_2, P_3, \ldots$, where $P_m = A$ is payable after m years if (x) is still alive. Discounting the amount A m years for interest and mortality is equivalent to multiplying A by v^m and $_m p_x$. This gives the present value of the mth annual payment as $A \cdot v^m \cdot _m p_x$. Summing over all possible m gives the result in the previous paragraph.

A variation of the above life annuity is a so-called *deferred life annuity*. The first annual amount A is payable at the end of the

$(n + 1)^{st}$ year, instead of at the end of the first year, if the annuitant is still alive. An application of this kind of annuity is in the provision of retirement benefits. Each year, the employer buys a deferred life annuity for each employee, so that the employee will receive a whole life annuity after retirement. The n in the above description is the number of years between the current age of an employee and retirement age.

How do we calculate the present value of such a deferred life annuity? Clearly one easy way is to set the lower limit of the summation in the present value of the whole life annuity at $m = n + 1$. Another way is to use the concept of mortality discount. A life annuity to (x) deferred n years is the same as a whole life annuity to $(x + n)$. Now if we discount the present value of a whole life annuity to $(x + n)$ backward n years for interest and mortality, we should obtain the present value of a life annuity to (x) deferred n years. Using this approach, the present value is then

$$v^n \cdot {}_n p_x \cdot A \sum_{m=1}^{\infty} v^m \cdot {}_m p_{x+n}.$$

The reader will be asked to prove that these two approaches give the same present value.

Exercises

5. What is the present value of a whole life annuity of $100 to a person at age 80?

6. A person is now retiring at age 65. She is entitled to an annual pension of $12,000, payable at the end of each year until she dies. What is the present value of the pension payments?

7. Use the information in **Exercise 6**, except that the person is now at age 60, i.e. she will not retire until 5 years later. What is the present value of her pension payments?

8. A person is entitled to his full Social Security benefits at age 65. His company tries to encourage him to retire early at age 60 by promising to pay an annual amount equal to his future Social Security benefits between ages 60 and 65. Such an arrangement is called a Social Security *bridge*, because its payments form a bridge from the time of retirement to the time when Social Security benefits are payable. Assume, for simplicity, that the benefits are $9,000 per year payable at the end of each year. What is the present value of this Social Security bridge when the employee is at age 60?

9. Show that the two approaches suggested in the last paragraph of this section give the same result.

5. Life Insurance

A *whole life insurance* policy provides that if a person dies, then his/her beneficiary will receive a certain death benefit, called the *face amount* of the policy. For simplicity, we assume that the benefit is paid at the end of the year of death. Suppose that the person is currently at age x, and the face amount is A. What is the present value of the death benefit? Let us observe that the benefit is payable n years later if (x) survives $(n-1)$ years but dies before the end of the nth year. This event has a probability of $_{n-1}p_x \cdot _1q_{x+n-1}$. Thus, with this probability, the present value of the death benefit is $A \cdot v^n$. Summing over all n, we have the (expected) present value

$$\sum_{n=1}^{\infty} A \cdot v^n \cdot _{n-1}p_x \cdot _1q_{x+n-1}.$$

A variation of the whole life insurance policy is a *term life insurance* policy, which only insures a person for a finite period of time, called the term of the policy. If the insured person does not die within this period, no death benefit will be payable when the person eventually dies. With the assumptions in the previous paragraph, and a term of m years, the only adjustment necessary in the present value summation is the change in the upper limit from ∞ to m.

We notice that the mortality discount factor $_np_x$ is not applicable here. Such a discount factor is used when a payment is made contingent upon survival, and we discount because there is a probability that it need not be paid because of prior death. In insurance, a payment is made contingent upon death, and so the discount factor $_np_x$ should not be used.

Exercises
10. What is the present value of a whole life insurance policy with a face amount of $10,000 for a person currently at age 50?

11. What is the present value of a term life insurance policy with a face amount of $10,000 and a term of 10 years, for a person currently at age 50?

12. Prove that, in general, the present value of a term life insurance policy is not greater than the present value of a whole life insurance policy for the same person and the same face amount.

6. Generalizations

Our discussions are based on payments being made at the end of a year. In reality, most annuities are payable more frequently than annually; for example, Social Security benefits and pension payments are payable monthly, and insurance death benefits are payable after death as soon as administratively possible. Furthermore, annuity and insurance policies are very often packed with other features. Interested readers are referred to [Bowers 1987] and [Jordan 1967] for these variations.

Our exercises are based on a very simple mortality assumption. The study of mortality is a complicated topic by itself, and data are collected and analyzed continuously to update mortality assumptions.

In this module, we have concentrated on the expected present value. Obviously, the variance is also an important quantity to consider, because it gives us an idea of the magnitude of deviations. Interested readers are again referred to [Bowers 1987] for details.

7. Answers to Exercises

1. $_{40}q_{20} = 1/2$.

2. $_{50}p_{20} - _{60}p_{20} = 1/8$.

3. $\$100 \cdot v^{10} \cdot _{10}p_{40} = \$100 \cdot (1.07)^{-10} \cdot \left(\frac{50}{60}\right) = \$42.36$.

4. $\$40,000 \cdot v^8 \cdot _8p_{10} = \$40,000 \cdot (1.07)^{-8} \cdot \left(\frac{82}{90}\right) = \$21,211$.

5. $\$100 \sum_{m=1}^{\infty} v^m \cdot _mp_{80} = \$100 \sum_{m=1}^{20}(1.07)^{-m} \cdot \left(\dfrac{20 - m}{20}\right) = \$619$.

   Note that the upper limit is 20 because a person must die by age 100 in our model.

6. $\$12,000 \sum_{m=1}^{35} v^m \cdot _mp_{65} = \$12,000 \sum_{m=1}^{35}(1.07)^{-m} \cdot \left(\dfrac{35 - m}{35}\right) =$
   $\$103,572$.

7. $\$12,000 \cdot (1.07)^{-5} \cdot _5p_{60} \sum_{m=1}^{35}(1.07)^{-m} \cdot \left(\dfrac{35 - m}{35}\right) = (1.07)^{-5} \cdot$
   $\left(\frac{35}{40}\right) \cdot \$103,572 = \$64,615$.

8. $\$9,000 \sum_{m=1}^{5} v^m \cdot _mp_{60} = \$9,000 \sum_{m=1}^{5}(1.07)^{-m} \cdot \left(\dfrac{40 - m}{40}\right) =$
   $\$34,259$.

This is an example of a temporary life annuity, because it lasts for at most 5 years.

9. $A\sum_{m=n+1}^{\infty} v^m \cdot {}_m p_x = A\sum_{l=1}^{\infty} v^{l+n} \cdot {}_{l+n} p_x$, where $l = m - n$

$$= A\sum_{l=1}^{\infty} v^l \cdot v^n \cdot {}_n p_x \cdot {}_l p_{x+n} = v^n \cdot {}_n p_x \cdot$$

$A\sum_{l=1}^{\infty} v^l \cdot {}_l p_{x+n}$.

10. $\$10,000 \sum_{n=1}^{50} v^n \cdot {}_{n-1} p_{50} \cdot {}_1 q_{49+n}$

$= \$10,000 \sum_{n=1}^{50} (1.07)^{-n}$

$\cdot \left(\dfrac{51 - n}{50} \right) \cdot \left(1 - \dfrac{50 - n}{51 - n} \right)$

$= \$10,000 \sum_{n=1}^{50} (1.07)^{-n} \cdot \frac{1}{50} =$

$\$2,760.$

11. $\$10,000 \sum_{n=1}^{10} (1.07)^{-n} \cdot \frac{1}{50} = \$1,405.$

12. (The present value of whole life insurance)

$-$(the present value of term life insurance)

$= \sum_{n=m+1}^{\infty} A \cdot v^n \cdot {}_{n-1} p_x \cdot {}_1 q_{x+n-1} \geq 0,$

because each summand ≥ 0.

(Note: The sums can be found by calculators or by series manipulation.)

References

Bowers, N. L., Jr., et al. 1987. *Actuarial Mathematics*. Itasca, IL: Society of Actuaries.

Jordan, C. W. 1967. *Life Contingencies*. Society of Actuaries.

Kellison, S. G. 1970. *The Theory of Interest*. Homewood, IL: Richard D. Irwin.

Ng, H. K. 1987. Simple Mortality Functions. UMAP Modules on Undergraduate Mathematics and Its Applications: Module 681. Reprinted in *The UMAP Journal* 8(3) (1987):237–250, and also in *UMAP Modules: Tools for Teaching* 1987, 279–292. Arlington, MA: COMAP, Inc.

About the Authors

Ho Kuen Ng received his B.S. from the University of Hong Kong and his Ph.D. degree from the University of California, Berkeley. In addition to teaching at San Jose State University, he spends some of his time doing actuarial work. His major interests are algebra, operations research, and actuarial science.

UMAP

Modules in
Undergraduate
Mathematics
and its
Applications

Published in
cooperation with
the Society for
Industrial and
Applied
Mathematics, the
Mathematical
Association of
America, the
National Council of
Teachers of
Mathematics, the
American
Mathematical
Association of Two-
Year Colleges, The
Institute of
Management
Sciences, and the
American Statistical
Association.

Module 703

Finding Vintage Concentrations in a Sherry Solera

Rhodes Peele
Jack MacQueen

Applications of Calculus to Wine-making

COMAP, Inc. 60 Lowell Street, Arlington, MA (617) 641-2600

INTERMODULAR DESCRIPTION SHEET:	UMAP Unit 703
TITLE:	Finding Vintage Concentrations in a Sherry Solera
AUTHOR:	Rhodes Peele Dept. of Mathematics Auburn University at Montgomery Montgomery, AL 36117–35 and John T. MacQueen 201 Valley Park Drive Chapel Hill, NC 27514
MATHEMATICAL FIELD:	Calculus
APPLICATION FIELD:	Wine-making
TARGET AUDIENCE:	Students who have studied infinite series and want to see a nontrivial physical application

ABSTRACT:

This Module models the solera method of making sherry and demonstrates that the method results in a mixture whose composition changes slowly with time and in which no single vintage constitutes a substantial fraction of the whole.

This Module is appropriate for a variety of courses. For example, it could serve as an introduction to mathematical modeling, or as enrichment material for a second-semester or third-quarter calculus course.

To derive full value from the Module, students should work as many exercises as they can without looking at the solutions. The exercises are designed to be challenging and to show the power and utility of calculus. It may be appropriate in certain situations for the instructor to provide hints for some of them. The more elaborate exercises could be the basis for oral presentations by students in an undergraduate seminar on mathematical modeling.

PREREQUISITES:

1. Ability to comprehend proofs by mathematical induction.
2. Familiarity with binomial coefficients and their manipulation.
3. Knowledge of the elementary theory of infinite sequences and series.

©Copyright 1991 by COMAP, Inc. All rights reserved.

COMAP, Inc., 60 Lowell St., Arlington, MA 02174 (617) 641–2600

Finding Vintage Concentrations in a Sherry Solera

Rhodes Peele
Dept. of Mathematics
Auburn University at Montgomery
Montgomery, AL 36117–35

John T. MacQueen
201 Valley Park Drive
Chapel Hill, NC 27514

Table of Contents

MODULES AND MONOGRAPHS IN UNDERGRADUATE
MATHEMATICS AND ITS APPLICATIONS (UMAP) PROJECT

The goal of UMAP is to develop, through a community of users and developers, a system of instructional modules in undergraduate mathematics and its applications to be used to supplement existing courses and from which complete courses may eventually be built.

The Project was guided by a National Advisory Board of mathematicians, scientists, and educators. UMAP was funded by a grant from the National Science Foundation and is now supported by the Consortium for Mathematics and Its Applications (COMAP), Inc., a non-profit corporation engaged in research and development in mathematics education.

COMAP Staff

Paul J. Campbell	Editor
Solomon Garfunkel	Executive Director, COMAP
Laurie W. Aragon	Development Director
Philip A. McGaw	Production Manager
Roland Cheyney	Project Manager
Laurie M. Holbrook	Copy Editor
Robin Altomonte	Administrative Asst./Distribution
Dale Horn	Design Assistant

1. The Solera Method

Sherry, unlike many other wines, is never bottled as a single-vintage wine, i.e, one produced entirely from grapes grown in a single year; nor is it a blend of wines from two or three vintages. Rather, it is a complex mixture resulting from the gradual withdrawal of older wines with compensating introduction of newly-made wine. This procedure results in a mixture whose composition changes slowly with time and in which no single vintage ever constitutes more than a small fraction of the whole.

We shall describe this process in detail in order to develop a mathematical model to calculate the composition of the mixture as a function of time.

The apparatus used is called a *solera*[1] and the entire procedure is sometimes referred to as the *solera method*. The apparatus consists of a series of barrels arranged one above the next, with older wines in the lowest tier and younger ones in the topmost. There are usually at least four tiers and sometimes as many as eight.

Sherry to be bottled is withdrawn from the lowest barrel; generally no more than one-third of a barrel is taken. That barrel is refilled from the one immediately above, which in turn is refilled from the barrel above it. This process is repeated until all the lower tiers are again full; then the topmost tier is topped off with new wine. The entire assembly then rests undisturbed until the next draw-down. We shall assume that the interval between draw-downs is sufficient for the contents of each barrel to become thoroughly mixed to a uniform composition. In our discussion we shall assume the usual custom of annual draw-downs, so that a wine that has been in the solera for n years will have undergone n transfers.

2. A Simple Model

In order to follow the distribution of a particular new wine W through the solera, let us assume for simplicity that the top tier is *completely* filled with W, and that the fraction drawn down each time is $\frac{1}{2}$.

Designate the year in which W is introduced as year 0 and the subsequent years (transfers) as $1, 2, \ldots, n$. Further, number the tiers $0, 1, \ldots, K$ *from the top down*. Let $f(n, k)$ be the fraction of wine in tier k which has been in the solera for n years and hence has undergone n transfers.

---

[1] According to [Bespaloff 1980], the term *solera* properly refers only to the lowest tier. The topmost, into which new wines are introduced, is the *añada* (from the Spanish *añadir*, meaning "to fill"), and the intermediate tiers comprise the *criadero* (or "nursery"). Nevertheless, in ordinary usage *solera* is usually taken to mean the entire apparatus.

Furthermore, in a large sherry house each tier may contain a thousand or more barrels. Tiers may not be actually stacked one above the next; they may even be stored in different cellars. Traditionally, however, and in small operations today, tiers are so arranged. In any case, the system of partial withdrawal and successive blending is as described.

We have $f(0,0) = 1$. After the first transfer, we have $f(1,0) = \frac{1}{2}$, $f(1,1) = \frac{1}{2}$. A second transfer moves $\frac{1}{2}\frac{1}{2} = \frac{1}{4}$ barrel of $\mathcal{W}$ from tier 1 to tier 2 (leaving behind $\frac{1}{4}$ barrel of $\mathcal{W}$), and also transfers $\frac{1}{4}$ barrel of $\mathcal{W}$ from tier 0 to tier 1 (leaving behind $\frac{1}{4}$ barrel of $\mathcal{W}$), so that we have

$$f(2,0) = \frac{1}{4}, \quad f(2,1) = \frac{2}{4}, \quad \text{and} \quad f(2,2) = \frac{1}{4}. \tag{1}$$

A repetition of this process yields

$$f(3,0) = \frac{1}{8}, \quad f(3,1) = \frac{3}{8}, \quad f(3,2) = \frac{3}{8}, \quad \text{and} \quad f(3,3) = \frac{1}{8}.$$

(The details of this step comprise **Exercise 1**.)

We may now generalize these relationships by observing that in year n (in the nth transfer) tier k will retain half of its contents from the previous year, i.e., $f(n-1,k)/2$, and receive half of the previous year's contents of the tier above it (tier $k-1$), so that

$$f(n,k) = \frac{f(n-1,k)}{2} + \frac{f(n-1,k-1)}{2}. \tag{2}$$

From this result[2], along with the well-known recurrence formula for binomial coefficients,

$$\binom{n}{k} = \binom{n-1}{k} + \binom{n-1}{k-1} \tag{3}$$

and the fact that $f(0,0) = 1 = \binom{0}{0}$, we may now infer by mathematical induction (**Exercise 2**) that

$$f(n,k) = \binom{n}{k}\frac{1}{2^n}, \quad \text{for } k \leq n. \tag{4}$$

The well-known relationship

$$\sum_{k=0}^{n} \binom{n}{k}\frac{1}{2^n} = 1$$

is reflected in the present model by the fact that as long as a particular wine remains in the solera, its various fractions, however distributed, must add to 1.

---

[2]In analyzing a given solera we are primarily interested in the composition of the bottom tier, for which $k = K$. We may imagine a equivalent *virtual* solera that has as many tiers as there have been transfers, i.e., $k_{\max} = n$. Clearly, in this case **(2)** must always apply. Our conclusions concerning the composition of the tier of interest ($k = K$) that actually supplies the finished product will not be affected by the fact that the virtual tiers do not exist.

3. A More Realistic Model

The situation becomes slightly more complicated with a more realistic value, such as one-fourth, for the fraction drawn down each year. We still assume that the top tier is completely filled with a single wine in year zero. Each tier will now retain three-fourths of its contents at each transfer and (except for the top tier) will receive one-fourth of the contents of the tier above. Using the formulas

$$f(0,0) = 1;$$

$$f(1,0) = \frac{3}{4}f(0,0), \ f(1,1) = \frac{1}{4}f(0,0);$$

$$f(2,0) = \frac{3}{4}f(1,0), \ f(2,1) = \frac{3}{4}f(1,1) + \frac{1}{4}f(1,0), \ f(2,2) = \frac{1}{4}f(1,1);$$

$$f(3,0) = \frac{3}{4}f(2,0), \ f(3,1) = \frac{3}{4}f(2,1) + \frac{1}{4}f(2,0)$$

$$f(3,2) = \frac{3}{4}f(2,2) + \frac{1}{4}f(2,1), \ f(3,3) = \frac{1}{4}f(2,2)$$

we compute the values

$$f(0,0) = 1;$$

$$f(1,0) = \frac{3}{4}, \ f(1,1) = \frac{1}{4};$$

$$f(2,0) = \frac{9}{16}, \ f(2,1) = \frac{6}{16}, \ f(2,2) = \frac{1}{16};$$

$$f(3,0) = \frac{27}{64}, \ f(3,1) = \frac{27}{64}, \ f(3,2) = \frac{9}{64}, \ f(3,3) = \frac{1}{64}. \tag{5}$$

If instead of one-fourth we choose a fractional draw-down of p, with $0 < p < 1$, we obtain

$$f(0,0) = 1;$$

$$f(1,0) = (1-p)f(0,0) = 1 - p, \quad f(1,1) = pf(0,0) = p;$$

$$f(2,0) = (1-p)f(1,0) = (1-p)^2,$$

$$f(2,1) = pf(1,0) + (1-p)f(1,1) = 2(1-p)p,$$

$$f(2,2) = pf(1,1) = p^2. \tag{6}$$

At least for $n = 0, 1$ and 2, the value of $f(n,k)$ is the kth term in the binomial expansion of

$$\{(1-p) + p\}^n.$$

To show that this relation holds for all n, we use mathematical induction. Taking computation **(6)** as the basis step, we need only show that if the relationship is true when $n = n'$, it must also be true for $n = n' + 1$.

Assume that

$$f(n', k) = \binom{n'}{k} p^k (1 - p)^{n'-k}.$$

In the next transfer $(n = n' + 1)$, tier k will retain $1 - p$ of its content from year n' and receive p of the contents of tier $k - 1$ from year n'. Thus

$$f(n' + 1, k) = (1 - p)f(n', k) + pf(n', k - 1)$$

$$= (1 - p)\binom{n'}{k} p^k (1 - p)^{n'-k} + p\binom{n'}{k-1} p^{k-1}(1-p)^{n-(k-1)}$$

$$= p^k (1-p)^{(n'+1)-k}\left\{ \binom{n'}{k} + \binom{n'}{k-1} \right\}$$

$$= \binom{n'+1}{k} p^k (1-p)^{(n'+1)-k},$$

which is the desired result. Note that the computation is valid for integers $k = 0$ and $k = n' + 1$ if we adopt the familiar convention of defining $\binom{i}{j}$ to be zero for $j < 0$ and for $j > i$.

One further modification is needed. We have assumed thus far that initially the top barrel is completely filled with a single wine, i.e., $f(0,0) = 1$. In practice the top tier is only partly emptied by the draw-down, so only a fraction of a barrel of new wine is introduced. If the fraction drawn is p, we start with p barrels of new wine rather than one barrel, i.e., $f(0,0) = p$. Our final expression is thus

$$f(n, k) = \binom{n}{k} p^{k+1}(1-p)^{n-k}. \tag{7}$$

For the usual case of annual draw-downs, we now take note of an important characteristic of the solera. The number of transfers n that a particular wine has undergone will equal the number of years that the wine has been in the solera. This number, together with the value of p, completely determine the distribution of that wine throughout the solera.[3] Thus, for example, once the solera has been in operation for at least 10 years, the fraction of 10-year-old wine in the finished product (in tier K) remains constant. (For a five-tier solera, this fraction is given by $f(10,4)$.) In this sense the structure of the distribution of wines in the solera is stable, even though the wines in the

---

[3]Since $f(n, k)$ does depend as well on the value of p, we could have used the notation $f(n, k, p)$ to express this explicitly. We note that here f is a discrete function of n and k (since n and k are restricted to integral values) but is a continuous function of p. In fact, it is a differentiable function of p; and we take advantage of this fact in **Exercises 9** and **11**.

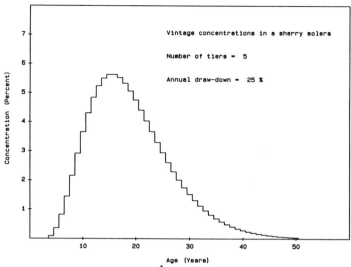

Figure 1. Vintage concentration as a function of age.

solera change from year to year. For example, the wine for which $n = 10$ in 1990 is obviously different from that for which $n = 10$ in 1995.

What will be the composition of the final product after many years of operation? Clearly, the youngest wine in tier K must have $n = K$. Since the lowest tier is exactly refilled after each draw-down, the fractional amounts from the youngest $(n = K)$ to the oldest $(n \to \infty)$ must add to 1. Thus we must have

$$\sum_{n=K}^{\infty} f(n,K) = \lim_{N \to \infty} \sum_{n=K}^{N} \binom{n}{K} p^{K+1}(1-p)^{n-K} = 1. \tag{8}$$

In **Exercises 9** and **10** we consider two proofs of this mathematical relationship which do not depend on the physical structure of our model.

To illustrate the results of the foregoing analysis, consider a five-tier solera $(K = 4)$ with a draw-down of one fourth $(p = \frac{1}{4})$ so that

$$f(n,4) = \binom{n}{4}\left(\frac{1}{4}\right)^5 \left(\frac{3}{4}\right)^{n-4}$$

which for purposes of calculation may be written

$$f(n,4) = \left(\frac{3}{4}\right)^{n-4} \frac{n(n-1)(n-2)(n-3)}{24576}.$$

Figure 1 shows the results of this calculation in the form of a histogram. Some important features of this figure are:

- Since a maximum is reached at $f(15,4) = f(16,4) \approx 0.0563$, no single year ever constitutes as much as 6% of the final blend.

Table 1.

Age Range (n_1 to n_2)	Accumulated Fraction in Range ($\sum_{n=n_1}^{n_2} f(n,4)$ as %)
0 – 9	7.81
10 – 19	50.70
20 – 29	31.70
30 – 39	8.19
40 – 49	1.39
50 or more	0.21

- The solera always retains a significant fraction of "older wines."

The second observation is illustrated in tabular form in **Table 1**.
In **Exercises 4–8** we offer an opportunity to verify the foregoing observations and to derive further properties of the sequences $f(n,k)$.

4.   Behavior of the Residual Terms

A particular solera can have been in operation for only a finite time (say n^* years). What then can be the significance of extending the sum in **(8)** beyond n^*? When a new solera is set up, it must be completely filled (except for a fraction p of the top tier) from existing stocks. The sherry used for this initial fill may itself be a mixture. In the absence of specific information concerning its composition, all we can do is to treat it as if it were a single wine. Hence $f(n,k)$ will be given by **(7)** for $n = 0, 1, 2, \ldots, n^*$, and the remainder $f_R(n^*, k)$ will represent the residual fraction of the initial fill :

$$f_R(n^*, k) = \sum_{n=n^*+1}^{\infty} f(n, k). \tag{9}$$

For small values of n^*, f_R will be large but must (on the basis of physical considerations) become smaller as n^* increases and in fact must approach zero as n^* increases without limit. For purposes of calculation, we may write

$$f_R(n^*, k) = 1 - \sum_{n=k}^{n^*} f(n, k) \tag{10}$$

and compute f_R in a term-by-term *subtraction* as values of $f(n, k)$ are computed from **(7)**.

This approach runs into a technical problem frequently encountered in floating-point calculations. Since only some fixed number of digits will be carried in each step, we reach a point at which $f(n,k)$ is so small that it is less than the roundoff error in earlier, much larger, terms. At this point f_R appears to become constant at a nonzero value. This behavior is shown in the second column of **Table 2**. Here f_R appears to stabilize at about 3.764×10^{-9} for $n^* \geq 150$. (These calculations were done retaining seven digits in each step). This fraction does represent a very small amount of sherry; about 8.48×10^{-4} cubic centimeters in a 225 liter ($\approx$ 60 gallon) barrel! For practical purposes we might simply choose to ignore it. On the other hand, the reduction of roundoff error is an important consideration in numerical analysis [Cheney and Kincaid 1980].

We now present two methods that minimize this problem.

Method 1. Add in reverse. Let $f(n,4) = 0$ for $n \geq 301$ and proceed as follows:

$$f_R(300,4) = 0,$$

$$f_R(299,4) = f_R(300,4) + f(300,4),$$

$$f_R(298,4) = f_R(299,4) + f(299,4),$$

$$\cdots$$

This method gives (to four significant figures) the values indicated in the last column of **Table 2** for $50 \leq n \leq 250$. We have essentially truncated from **(9)** those terms for which $n \geq 301$. In **Exercise 12** the total contribution of these terms is shown to be negligible for $n^* \leq 250$. Note that we add the retained terms in reverse order (i.e., from smallest to largest) to reduce roundoff error.

Method 2. Find a more amenable closed form. In an attempt to avoid both undesirable roundoff error and the large amount of numerical work involved in the above methods, we sought an alternative approach. We were able to show that

$$f_R(n^*, k) = \sum_{j=0}^{k} \binom{n^* + 1}{j} (1 - p)^{n^*+1-j} p^j. \tag{11}$$

A sum will still have to be calculated, but for a five-tier solera ($k = 4$) it will have *only five terms*, whatever the value of n. Use of **(11)** gives (to four significant figures) the values listed in the last column of **Table 2**, in agreement with Method 1 above, except, of course, for $f_R(300,4)$.

In finding **(11)** we employed a technique suggested by the proof of **(8)** which we present in **Exercise 9**. This derivation we present in guided form in **Exercise 11**.

5.   An Equivalent Stochastic Process [4]

Consider an infinite one-dimensional array of cells numbered $k = 0, 1, 2, \ldots$. Initially a marker is in cell $k = 0$. At each "tick of the clock," a message is received. With probability p the message is "Move the marker from its present position, k, to the next larger numbered cell, $k + 1$." With probability $1 - p$ the message is "leave the marker in its present cell." After n "ticks of the clock," what is the probability that the marker is in cell k?

In this case the "motion" of the marker may be described as the evolution of a stochastic process. Define a matrix of transition probabilities $P = (p_{ij})$, where the p_{ij} are constants such that $\sum_{j=0}^{\infty} p_{ij} = 1$, and p_{ij} is the conditional probability that if the system is in state i at "time" n, it will be in the state j at "time" $n+1$. Then $S^{(n+1)} = P \cdot S^{(n)}$, where the vector $S^{(n)} = \left(s_0^{(n)}, s_1^{(n)}, s_2^{(n)}, \ldots \right)$ and the components of $S^{(n+1)}$ are given by $s_j^{(n+1)} = \sum_{i=0}^{\infty} p_{ij} s_i^{(n)}$. For the system described above the p_{ij} are given by

$$p_{ij} = \begin{cases} 1 - p, & \text{for } i = j; \\ p, & \text{for } j = i + 1; \\ 0, & \text{otherwise} \end{cases}$$

Given an initial state vector $S^{(0)} = (s_0, s_1, \ldots, s_i, \ldots)$, we may obtain the state vector $S^{(n)}$ that gives the probability distribution after n "ticks of the clock" by multiplying $S^{(0)}$ n times by P. In the present case our initial state vector is

$$S^{(0)} = (1,\ 0,\ 0,\ 0,\ \ldots). \tag{12}$$

If $p = \frac{1}{4}$, multiplying by P^n will yield a series of state vectors $S^{(n)}$ whose components are the same as the $f(n, k)$ calculated in (5) above, i.e.,

$$S^{(0)} = (1,\ 0,\ 0,\ 0,\ \ldots)$$
$$S^{(1)} = (3/4,\ 1/4,\ 0,\ 0,\ \ldots)$$
$$S^{(2)} = (9/16,\ 6/16,\ 1/16,\ 0,\ \ldots)$$
$$S^{(3)} = (27/64,\ 27/64,\ 9/64,\ 1/64,\ \ldots)$$

$$\ldots \tag{13}$$

If, instead of (12), which is appropriate to the problem as stated, we take

$$S^{(0)} = (p,\ 0,\ 0,\ 0,\ \ldots),$$

we obtain a series of vectors whose components are given, similarly, by (7).

---

[4]This section may be omitted by readers who lack a background in probability theory.

It is easier to see the analogy to the solera problem if we assume that, initially, cell 0 contains not a single marker but a very large number of points (a number on the order of magnitude of the number of molecules in a barrel of sherry $\approx 10^{27}$). The components of $S^{(n)}$ thus calculated may then be interpreted as the *expected number* of these points in cell k after n transitions.

6.   Concluding Observations

Our analysis of the solera process shows in detail that the solera method, which must have been devised originally from empirical considerations and established by tradition, achieves its desired objectives. The calculations in the text and Exercises indicate the usual values of parameters k and p do indeed result in a blend having the desired characteristics: Wine from no one year ever constitutes more than a small part of the whole, and the resulting blend always retains wine from a broad spectrum of harvests.

We hope that the reader will have found the various mathematical techniques which we have employed both interesting and instructive and will have realized some of the ways in which numerical computations can be misleading unless care is taken in their design and organization.

7. Exercises

1. Making use of the values of $f(2, k)$ already found in **(1)**, calculate $f(3, k)$ for $k = 0, 1, 2, 3$.

2. Deduce **(4)** from **(2)**, **(3)** and the initial condition $f(0,0) = 1$.

3. Using **(7)**, derive the recurrence relation

$$f(n + 1, k) = (1 - p)\frac{n + 1}{n + 1 - k} f(n, k) \qquad (n \geq k).$$

4. Let k be fixed. Using the recurrence relation derived in **Exercise 3**, find the maximum value of $f(n, k)$ over all $n \geq k$, and find an index n that achieves this maximum value.

5. Show that for fixed p and k, the maximum value $f(n, k)$ in **Exercise 4** is achieved either once or twice, and give a simple rule to determine which is the case.

6. For fixed p and k, let $M(p, k)$ denote the maximum value of $f(n, k)$ for $n \geq k$ as determined in **Exercise 4**. In this problem we derive a simplified formula for $M(p, k)$ at the cost of introducing a small quantitative error.

   a) Using the expression for $M(p, k)$ you derived in **Exercise 4**, the factorial formula for binomial coefficients, *Stirling's approximation* for factorials,

$$m! \approx \sqrt{2\pi m}\left(\frac{m}{e}\right)^m,$$

   and the approximation $\lfloor k/p \rfloor \approx k/p$, show that

$$M(p, k) \approx \frac{p}{\sqrt{2\pi(1 - p)k}}.$$

   Here $\lfloor \; \rfloor$ denotes the "greatest integer" or "floor" function defined by

$$\lfloor x \rfloor = \max\{n \mid n \leq x \text{ and } n \text{ is an integer}\}.$$

   b) Using a pocket calculator, compare the "exact" value for $M(p, k)$ as determined in **Exercise 4** with its approximate value from **Exercise 6a**, for the four parameter sets for p and k listed in **Exercise 8** below. Determine the relative percent of error,

$$\frac{\left| M(p, k) - \frac{p}{\sqrt{2\pi(1-p)k}} \right|}{M(p, k)} \times 100\%,$$

for all four situations. (This should give you some feeling for how accurate the approximation is for reasonable values of p and k.)

c) On the basis of parts **(a)** and **(b)**, complete the following rule of thumb by filling in the blank with the smallest integer that makes the statement true: "In an established solera with at least four tiers and a draw-down of not more that $\frac{1}{3}$, the largest vintage in the final product never accounts for more than ___% of its total volume."

7. Write a BASIC program that accepts as input an arbitrary p with $0 < p < 1$ and nonnegative integer k, and generates a table like **Table 1**.

8. Using a graphics software package for a computer-driven plotter, write a program that accepts as input an arbitrary p with $0 < p < 1$ and non-negative integer k, and generates a histogram like **Figure 1**. Run the program, letting **a)** $p = 0.2, k = 3$; **b)** $p = 0.25, k = 3$; **c)** $p = 0.2, k = 4$; **d)** $p = 0.3, k = 4$.

9. Prove **(8)** by mathematical induction, carrying out these steps:

a) Use the substitution $x = 1 - p$ to transform **(8)** into the Maclaurin series

$$\sum_{n=k}^{\infty} \binom{n}{k} x^{n-k} = \left(\frac{1}{1-x}\right)^{k+1}. \tag{14}$$

b) Prove by mathematical induction that **(14)** is valid for $-1 < x < 1$ and $k = 0, 1, 2, \ldots$. Base your inductive step on the fact that a convergent power series can be differentiated term by term.

10. This exercise develops an alternative proof of **(8)** which avoids using differentiation. We begin as in **Exercises 9a**, so that our task is to establish the inductive step of **Exercise 9b** by a different method.

a) Use the ratio test to show that for any integer $k \geq 0$, the series $\sum_{n=k}^{\infty} \binom{n}{k} x^{n-k}$ converges for $|x| < 1$. Denote the sum by S_k.

b) Using **(3)**, show that for any positive integer k, $S_k = x S_k + S_{k-1}$.

c) Conclude by mathematical induction that **(14)** holds for all nonnegative integers k if $-1 < x < 1$.

11. "Rediscover" and then prove **(11)** by carrying out the following steps:

a) We seek to evaluate the sum

$$f_R(n^*) \;=\; \sum_{n=n^*+1}^{\infty} f(n,k) \;=\; \sum_{n=n^*+1}^{\infty} \binom{n}{k} p^{k+1}(1-p)^{n-k} \tag{15}$$

for $0 < p < 1$. Begin as in **Exercise 9**, substituting x for $1 - p$, and also define $m = n^* + 1$. Show that **(15)** is then transformed into

$$\frac{f_R(m-1)}{(1-x)^{k+1}} = \sum_{n=m}^{\infty} \binom{n}{k} x^{n-k}. \tag{16}$$

This reduces **Exercise 11** to summing the right-hand side of **(16)**.

b) Before we can apply mathematical induction, we must make an informed guess of what the sum in **(16)** should be. (This difficulty did not arise in **Exercise 9**, because we know from physical considerations that the sum of **(8)** has to be 1.) We consider small values of k, starting with 0. Show that

$$\sum_{n=m}^{\infty} \binom{n}{0} x^{n-0} = \frac{x^m}{1-x}. \tag{17}$$

c) Show by differentiating both sides of **(17)** that

$$\sum_{n=m}^{\infty} \binom{n}{1} x^{n-1} = \frac{mx^{m-1}}{1-x} + \frac{x^m}{(1-x)^2}. \tag{18}$$

d) By differentiating a second time, and then dividing both sides by 2, show that

$$\sum_{n=m}^{\infty} \binom{n}{2} x^{n-2} =$$

$$\binom{m}{2}\frac{x^{m-2}}{1-x} + \binom{m}{1}\frac{x^{m-1}}{(1-x)^2} + \binom{m}{0}\frac{x^m}{(1-x)^3} \tag{19}$$

e) Identify the pattern suggested by **(17)**, **(18)** and **(19)**, and show by mathematical induction that this pattern persists for all integers $k \geq 0$.

f) Take the formula you derived in part **e** for the sum

$$\sum_{n=m}^{\infty} \binom{n}{k} x^{n-k}$$

and back-substitute $1 - p$ for x and $n^* + 1$ for m to obtain formula **(11)**.

12. It is customary to say that the floating-point number $m \times 10^{-c}$ ($1 \leq m < 10$, c an integer) *approximates* the real number r *to an accuracy of d digits* (or *significant figures*) if

$$|r - (m \times 10^{-c})| < 5 \times 10^{-(c+d)}.$$

If the context makes clear that r is the number that $m \times 10^{-c}$ approximates, we simply say that $m \times 10^{-c}$ is *accurate to d significant figures*.[5]

Table 2.

n^*	f_R by formula (10)	f_R by Methods 1 and 2
50	1.706×10^{-3}	1.706×10^{-3}
75	6.008×10^{-6}	6.005×10^{-6}
100	1.752×10^{-8}	1.375×10^{-8}
150	3.764×10^{-9}	3.802×10^{-14}
200	3.764×10^{-9}	6.685×10^{-20}
250	3.764×10^{-9}	9.146×10^{-26}
300	3.764×10^{-9}	1.067×10^{-31} (Method 2)

In this exercise we show, without making use of **Method 2**, that the values obtained in **Table 2** for $n^* \leq 250$ by **Method 1** are accurate to four significant figures. This amounts to showing that the *truncation error*[6] represented by $\sum_{n=301}^{\infty} f(n, 4)$ is less than 5×10^{-30}. The idea is to compare this series of truncated terms with a convergent geometric series that has slightly larger terms.

a) Show, by iterating the recurrence in **Exercise 3**, that if n, k and m are positive integers with $n \geq k$, then

$$f(n + m, k) =$$

$$(1 - p)^m \left(\frac{n + 1}{n - k + 1} \right) \left(\frac{n + 2}{n - k + 2} \right) \cdots \left(\frac{n + m}{n - k + m} \right) f(n, k)$$

$$\leq (1 - p)^m \left(\frac{n + 1}{n - k + 1} \right)^m f(n, k).$$

---

[5]Suppose $m \times 10^{-c}$ has been shown to approximate r to an accuracy of d digits (in the sense just defined), but the mantissa m has more than d digits, say $m = m_1.m_2m_3 \ldots m_e$ with $e > d$. Let $\mu = \mu_1.\mu_2\mu_3 \ldots \mu_d$ be m rounded off to d digits. Does it follow that $\mu \times 10^{-c}$ also approximates r to an accuracy of d digits? No, because the two errors $r - (m \times 10^{-c})$ and $(\mu \times 10^{-c}) - (m \times 10^{-c})$ might be of the same sign. In this situation the two given inequalities $|r - (m \times 10^{-c})| < 5 \times 10^{-(c+d)}$ and $|(\mu \times 10^{-c}) - (m \times 10^{-c})| < 5 \times 10^{-(c+d)}$ do *not* ensure that $|r - (\mu \times 10^{-c})| < 5 \times 10^{-(c+d)}$. Nevertheless, it is common practice to misuse language slightly and say that $\mu \times 10^{-c}$ approximates r to d decimal digits if $m \times 10^{-c}$ does.

[6]*Roundoff error* in the evaluation of $\sum_{n=n^*}^{300} f(n, 4)$ is not a serious concern, since

- the individual terms $f(n, 4)$ were computed to an accuracy of *seven* decimal digits to reduce roundoff error accumulation;

- since the terms in the sum are all positive, we avoid subtracting nearly equal floating-point numbers;

- the terms are added in reverse order (from smallest to largest), thereby assuring that during the course of the calculation the accumulated subtotal and the next term to be added have nearly equal orders of magnitude.

b) Let N and K be fixed positive integers such that $N + 1 > K/p$, and define

$$R = (1 - p)\left(\frac{N+1}{N+K-1}\right).$$

Show that

$$\sum_{n=N}^{\infty} f(n, K) < \frac{f(N, K)}{1 - R}$$

by comparing the left-hand side with the convergent geometric series

$$\sum_{m=0}^{\infty} f(N, K)R^m.$$

c) Show that

$$\sum_{n=301}^{\infty} f(n, 4) < 1.12 \times 10^{-31}$$

by choosing $N = 301$, $K = 4$ and $p = \frac{1}{4}$ in part **(b)**. Conclude that the entries in **Table 2** obtained by **Method 1** are certainly accurate to four significant figures.

d) In part **(c)** we exploited the inequality

$$\sum_{n=N}^{\infty} f(n, K) < \frac{f(N, K)}{1 - R}$$

by choosing $N = 301$ and showing that for $n^* \leq 250$, the second sum in

$$f(n^*) = \sum_{n=n^*}^{300} f(n, 4) + \sum_{n=301}^{\infty} f(n, 4)$$

is much smaller than the first sum. Another way to use this inequality is simply to choose $N = n^*$. This gives the loose upper bound

$$f_R(n^*) \leq \frac{f(n^*, K)}{1 - R},$$

which nevertheless is usually sharp enough to identify the *order of magnitude* of $f_R(n^*)$.

Tabulate $f(n^*, 4)/(1 - R)$ for $p = \frac{1}{4}$ and $n^* = 50, 75, 100, 150, 200, 250$, and see how well these values compare with the right-hand column of **Table 2**.

13. Write a BASIC program that accepts as input an arbitrary p, with $0 < p < 1$, and integers k and n^*, such that $0 \leq k \leq n^*$, and computes $f_R(n^*)$ by each of the following three methods :

a) formula **(10)** applied naively as in the second column of **Table 2**;

b) **Method 1**;

c) **Method 2**.

14

8.   Solutions to the Exercises

1. We are given that $f(2,0) = \frac{1}{4}$, $f(2,1) = \frac{2}{4}$, $f(2,2) = \frac{1}{4}$. In the next transfer tier 0 loses half of its contents, while tier 3 receives one-half the contents of tier 2. Thus $f(3,0) = f(3,3) = \frac{1}{2}\frac{1}{4} = \frac{1}{8}$. Tier 1 receives one-half the contents of tier 0 while retaining one-half of its former contents. Thus $f(3,1) = \frac{1}{2}\frac{1}{4} + \frac{1}{2}\frac{2}{4} = \frac{3}{8}$. Tier 2 receives one-half the contents of tier 1, again retaining one-half its previous contents, thus $f(3,2) = \frac{1}{2}\frac{2}{4} + \frac{1}{2}\frac{1}{4} = \frac{3}{8}$.

2. For integers n and k with $n \geq 0$, define $\binom{n}{k}$ to be zero for $k > n$ and for $k < 0$, and in the usual way for $0 \leq k \leq n$. It is easily checked that **(3)** remains true for all integers n and k with $n > 0$ if we use this extended definition for $\binom{n}{k}$. Moreover, we already know that **(4)** is true for all integers k if $n = 0, 1, 2$ or 3. Let n' be any nonnegative integer for which **(4)** is true for all integers k. Then from **(2)** and **(3)**,

$$f(n'+1, k) = \frac{f(n', k)}{2} + \frac{f(n', k-1)}{2}$$

$$= \frac{1}{2}\binom{n'}{k}\frac{1}{2^{n'}} + \frac{1}{2}\binom{n'}{k-1}\frac{1}{2^{n'}}$$

$$= \binom{n'+1}{k}\frac{1}{2^{n'+1}}.$$

Therefore **(4)** is true for all integers k if $n = n'+1$. It follows the principle of mathematical induction that **(4)** is true for all integers n and k with $n \geq 0$.

3. We have

$$\frac{f(n+1, k)}{f(n, k)} = \frac{\binom{n+1}{k}}{\binom{n}{k}} \frac{p(1-p)^{n+1-k}p^k}{p(1-p)^{n-k}p^k}$$

$$= (1-p)\frac{(n+1)!}{k!\,(n+1-k)!}\frac{k!\,(n-k)!}{n!} = (1-p)\frac{n+1}{n+1-k}.$$

4. For a given n, $f(n+1, k) > f(n, k)$ is equivalent to each of the following:

$$(1-p)\frac{n+1}{n+k-1} > 1 \quad ; \quad 1-p > 1 - \frac{k}{n+1} \quad ; \quad n+1 < \frac{k}{p}.$$

Similarly, $f(n+1, k) \leq f(n, k)$ is equivalent to $n+1 \geq k/p$. Thus, if we choose $n = \lfloor k/p \rfloor$, where $\lfloor\ \rfloor$ is the greatest integer or floor function, then the terms of the sequence will satisfy

$$f(k, k) < f(k+1, k) < \cdots < f(n, k) \geq f(n+1, k) \geq f(n+2, k) \geq \cdots.$$

Table 3.

Solution to **Exercise 6b**.

p	k	$M(p,k) \times 100\%$	$\dfrac{p}{\sqrt{2\pi(1-p)k}} \times 100\%$	% error
0.2	3	5.00%	5.15%	3.00%
0.25	3	6.45%	6.65%	3.10%
0.2	4	4.36%	4.46%	2.29%
0.3	4	7.01%	7.15%	2.00%

The maximum term of the sequence is therefore

$$f(\lfloor k/p \rfloor, k) = \binom{\lfloor k/p \rfloor}{k} p^{k+1}(1-p)^{\lfloor k/p \rfloor - k}.$$

5. Continuing the argument in **Exercise 4**, we see that if the sequence achieves its maximum value more than once, then it must have a pair of consecutive equal terms, i.e., $f(n+1, k) = f(n, k)$ for some n. This is equivalent to $n + 1 = k/p$. In this event, k/p is an integer, and the two values of the index n for which $f(n, k)$ is maximized are $(k/p) - 1$ and k/p.

6. a) Set $q = 1 - p$. Then

$$\binom{\lfloor k/p \rfloor}{k} p^{k+1} q^{\lfloor k/p \rfloor - k} \approx$$

$$\frac{\sqrt{2\pi k/p}\left(\dfrac{k}{ep}\right)^{k/p}}{\sqrt{2\pi k}\left(\dfrac{k}{e}\right)^{k}\sqrt{2\pi q k/p}\left(\dfrac{qk}{ep}\right)^{qk/p}} \, p^{k+1} q^{qk/p} =$$

$$\sqrt{\frac{2\pi k/p}{2\pi k \cdot 2\pi q k/p}} \cdot \frac{\left(\dfrac{k}{e}\right)^{k/p}}{\left(\dfrac{k}{e}\right)^{k}\left(\dfrac{k}{e}\right)^{qk/p}} \cdot \frac{p^{qk/p}}{p^{k/p} \cdot q^{qk/p}} \cdot p^{k+1} \cdot q^{qk/p} =$$

$$\sqrt{\frac{1}{2\pi q k}} \cdot \frac{p^{k+1}}{p^k} = \frac{p}{\sqrt{2\pi q k}}.$$

b) See **Table 3**.

c) To maximize $\dfrac{p}{\sqrt{2\pi(1-p)k}}$ subject to $0 < p \leq \frac{1}{3}$ and $k \geq 3$, k an integer, one chooses $p = \frac{1}{3}$, $k = 3$ to get $\frac{1}{3\sqrt{4\pi}} = 0.09403\ldots$. Since $M(p,k) \approx \frac{p}{\sqrt{2\pi(1-p)k}}$, we are therefore reasonably confident (especially after **Exercise 6b**) that $M(p,k) \times 100\%$ can exceed 9% but not 10%. So the integer 10 should go in the blank.

7. See **Figure 2**.

8. See **Figure 3**.

9. **a)** Substituting x for $1 - p$ transforms **(8)** into

$$\sum_{n=k}^{\infty} (1 - x)^{k+1} \binom{n}{k} x^{n-k} = 1. \tag{20}$$

Since $(1 - x)^{k+1}$ does not involve the summation variable n, we can factor it out of the summation. Dividing both sides of **(20)** by this factor gives **(14)**. Note that for $0 < p < 1$ we have $|x| < 1$ (in fact, $0 < x < 1$).

b) **Basis step.** If $k = 0$, the series in **(14)** is geometric with constant ratio x and initial term 1. Since the constant ratio is less than 1 in absolute value, the series is convergent, and its sum is

$$\frac{\text{initial term}}{1 - \text{constant ratio}} = \frac{1}{1 - x}.$$

Inductive step. Let m be any nonnegative integer such that

$$\sum_{n=m}^{\infty} \binom{n}{m} x^{n-m} = \left(\frac{1}{1 - x}\right)^{m+1} \tag{21}$$

for $|x| < 1$. Differentiate both sides of **(21)**. Since the left-hand side is a convergent power series, we may compute its derivative term-by-term. Furthermore, we know from calculus that the derivative will have the same radius of convergence. Therefore

$$\frac{d}{dx} \sum_{n=m}^{\infty} \binom{n}{m} x^{n-m} = \sum_{n=m+1}^{\infty} \binom{n}{m} (n - m) x^{n-m-1}$$

$$= (m + 1) \sum_{n=m+1}^{\infty} \binom{n}{m} \frac{n - m}{m + 1} x^{n-(m+1)}$$

$$= (m + 1) \sum_{n=m+1}^{\infty} \binom{n}{m + 1} x^{n-(m+1)}$$

$$= \frac{d}{dx} \left(\frac{1}{1 - x}\right)^{m+1} = (m + 1) \left(\frac{1}{1 - x}\right)^{m+2}$$

for $|x| < 1$. Cancellation of the (nonzero) factor $m + 1$ gives

$$\sum_{n=m+1}^{\infty} \binom{n}{m + 1} x^{n-(m+1)} = \left(\frac{1}{1 - x}\right)^{m+2}$$

for $|x| < 1$, thereby completing the inductive step.

17

```
2000 REM * This program is in GW-BASIC.
2100 CLS
2110 INPUT "p = ";P
2120 INPUT "k = ";K
2130 INPUT "Number of time intervals (e.g., for Table 1 of the
text, 6)";T
2200 DIM B(T) : DIM L(T) : DIM R(T - 1)
2210 PRINT "Enter the left endpoints of the time intervals that
are to form
2212 PRINT the table's left column (e.g., for Table 1 these are 0,
10, 20, 30, 40, 50)"
2220 FOR I = 1 TO T
2230 INPUT L(I)
2240 IF I > 1 THEN LET R(I - 1) = L(I) - 1
2250 NEXT I
2300 DIM A(L(T))
2310 FOR N = 0 TO K - 1 :  LET A(N) = 0 :  NEXT N
2320 LET A(K) = P^ (K + 1)
2330 LET B(T) = 1 - A(K)
2400 FOR N = K + 1 TO R(T - 1)
2410     LET A(N) = A(N - 1)*(1 - P)*N/(N - K)
2420     LET B(T) = B(T) - A(N)
2430 NEXT N
2500 FOR I = 1 TO T - 1
2510     LET B(I) = 0
2520     FOR J = L(I) TO R(I)
2530     LET B(I) = B(I) + A(J)
2540     NEXT J
2550 NEXT I
2600 PRINT "To print a table like Table 1 for the data you have
entered, hit 'return'."
2620 INPUT Z$
2630 CLS
2700 PRINT " Age range Accumulated fraction in range as %"
2710 FOR I = 1 TO T - 1
2715     PRINT L(I) TAB(6) "-" TAB(8) R(I),,
2720     PRINT USING "###.##";100!*B(I)
2730 NEXT I
2740 PRINT L(T);"or more",,
2750 PRINT USING "###.##";100!*B(T)
```

Figure 2. A solution to **Exercise 7.**

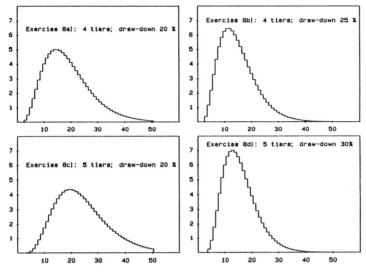

Figure 3. Solution to **Exercise 8**.

10. a) Let $a_n = \binom{n}{k} x^{n-k}$. Then

$$\lim_{n\to\infty} \left| \frac{a_{n+1}}{a_n} \right| = \lim_{n\to\infty} \frac{\left| \binom{n+1}{k} x^{n+1-k} \right|}{\left| \binom{n}{k} x^{n-k} \right|} = \lim_{n\to\infty} \frac{n+1}{n+1-k} |x|$$

$$= |x| < 1,$$

so the series converges.

b) We have

$$S_k = \sum_{n=k}^{\infty} \binom{n-1}{k} x^{n-k} + \sum_{n=k}^{\infty} \binom{n-1}{k-1} x^{n-k}$$

$$= x \sum_{n=k+1}^{\infty} \binom{n-1}{k} x^{n-k-1} + \sum_{m=k-1}^{\infty} \binom{m}{k-1} x^{m+1-k}$$

$$= x \sum_{m=k}^{\infty} \binom{m}{k} x^{m-k} + \sum_{m=k-1}^{\infty} \binom{m}{k-1} x^{m-(k-1)}$$

$$= x S_k + S_{k-1}.$$

c) Solving $S_k = x S_k + S_{k-1}$ for S_k, we get $S_k = S_{k-1}/(1-x)$. The inductive hypothesis is $S_{k-1} = 1/(1-x)^k$. Therefore $S_k = S_{k-1}/(1-x) = 1/(1-x)^{k+1}$, as was to be shown.

11. a) Similar to **Exercise 9a**. (Throughout **Exercise 11** we assume that $0 < p < 1$).

b) Similar to the basis step of **Exercise 9b**.

c) For the derivative of the left side of **(17)** we have

$$\frac{d}{dx} \sum_{n=m}^{\infty} \binom{n}{0} x^{n-0} = \frac{d}{dx} \sum_{n=m}^{\infty} x^n = \sum_{n=m}^{\infty} nx^{n-1} = \sum_{n=m}^{\infty} \binom{n}{1} x^{n-1};$$

for the right side,

$$\frac{d}{dx} \frac{x^m}{1-x} = \frac{(1-x)mx^{m-1} - x^m(-1)}{(1-x)^2} = \frac{mx^{m-1}}{1-x} + \frac{x^m}{(1-x)^2}.$$

Equating the two gives **(18)**.

d) For the derivative of the left side of **(18)**, we have

$$\frac{d}{dx} \sum_{n=m}^{\infty} \binom{n}{1} x^{n-1} = \frac{d}{dx} \sum_{n=m}^{\infty} nx^{n-1} = \sum_{n=m}^{\infty} n(n-1)x^{n-2}$$

$$= \sum_{n=m}^{\infty} 2\binom{n}{2} x^{n-2};$$

for the right side,

$$\frac{d}{dx} \left\{ \frac{mx^{m-1}}{1-x} + \frac{x^m}{(1-x)^2} \right\} =$$

$$\frac{(1-x)m(m-1)x^{m-2} - mx^{m-1}(-1)}{(1-x)^2}$$

$$+ \frac{(1-x)^2 mx^{m-1} - 2x^m(1-x)(-1)}{(1-x)^4}$$

$$= \frac{m(m-1)x^{m-2}}{1-x} + \frac{2mx^{m-1}}{(1-x)^2} + \frac{2x^m}{(1-x)^3}$$

$$= 2\binom{m}{2} \frac{x^{m-2}}{1-x} + 2\binom{m}{1} \frac{x^{m-1}}{(1-x)^2} + 2\binom{m}{0} \frac{x^{m-0}}{(1-x)^3}.$$

Equating the two and dividing by 2 gives **(19)**.

e) The pattern suggested by **(17)**, **(18)** and **(19)** is

$$\sum_{n=m}^{\infty} \binom{n}{k} x^{n-k} = \sum_{j=0}^{k} \binom{m}{j} \frac{x^{m-j}}{(1-x)^{k+1-j}} \quad \text{for } |x| < 1. \tag{22}$$

We prove by mathematical induction that **(22)** holds for all nonnegative integers k. The **basis step** of the argument has already been completed with **Exercise 11b** and (for good measure) **11c** and **11d**.

Inductive step. Let k be any fixed nonnegative integer for which **(22)** holds. As in **Exercises 11c** and **11d**, we differentiate both sides of **(22)** and equate the results. For the left side we get

$$\frac{d}{dx}\sum_{n=m}^{\infty}\binom{m}{k}x^{n-k} = \sum_{n=m}^{\infty}\binom{n}{k}(n-k)x^{n-k-1} =$$

$$\sum_{n=m}^{\infty}\binom{n}{k+1}(k+1)x^{n-(k+1)} = (k+1)\sum_{n=m}^{\infty}\binom{n}{k+1}x^{n-(k+1)}.$$

For the right side we must work much harder, but the special cases already considered in **Exercises 11c** and **11d** guide our efforts.[7]

$$\frac{d}{dx}\sum_{j=0}^{k}\binom{m}{j}\frac{x^{m-j}}{(1-x)^{k+1-j}} = \sum_{j=0}^{k}\binom{m}{j}\frac{d}{dx}\frac{x^{m-j}}{(1-x)^{k+1-j}} =$$

$$\sum_{j=0}^{k}\binom{m}{j}\frac{(1-x)^{k+1-j}(m-j)x^{m-j-1} + x^{m-j}(k+1-j)(1-x)^{k-j}}{(1-x)^{2k+2-2j}}$$

$$= \sum_{j=0}^{k}\binom{m}{j}\frac{(m-j)x^{m-j-1}}{(1-x)^{k+1-j}} + \sum_{j=0}^{k}\binom{m}{j}\frac{(k+1-j)x^{m-j}}{(1-x)^{k+2-j}}$$

$$= \sum_{j'=1}^{k+1}\binom{m}{j'-1}\frac{(m-j'+1)x^{m-j'}}{(1-x)^{k+2-j'}} + \sum_{j=0}^{k}\binom{m}{j}\frac{(k+1-j)x^{m-j}}{(1-x)^{k+2-j}}$$

$$= \sum_{j=1}^{k}\left\{(m-j+1)\binom{m}{j-1} + (k+1-j)\binom{m}{j}\right\}\frac{x^{m-j}}{(1-x)^{k+2-j}}$$

$$+ \binom{m}{0}\frac{(k+1)x^m}{(1-x)^{k+2}} + \binom{m}{k}\frac{(m-k)x^{m-k-1}}{1-x}$$

$$= \sum_{j=1}^{k}\left\{j\binom{m}{j} + (k+1-j)\binom{m}{j}\right\}\frac{x^{m-j}}{(1-x)^{k+2-j}}$$

$$+ \binom{m}{0}\frac{(k+1)x^m}{(1-x)^{k+2}} + \binom{m}{k+1}\frac{(k+1)x^{m-(k+1)}}{1-x}$$

$$= (k+1)\sum_{j=0}^{k+1}\binom{m}{j}\frac{x^{m-j}}{(1-x)^{k+2-j}}.$$

Equating the two derivatives now gives

---

[7]However, the computation is still difficult. The reader may find it helpful to work through one more special case ($k=3$) by computing the derivative of the right side of **(19)** before working through the general case.

$$(k+1)\sum_{n=m+1}^{\infty}\binom{n}{k+1}x^{n-(k+1)}=(k+1)\sum_{j=0}^{k+1}\binom{m}{j}\frac{x^{m-j}}{(1-x)^{k+2-j}},$$

and cancellation of the nonzero factor $k+1$ completes the inductive step.

f) We have shown that (22) holds for all nonnegative integers k if $|x|<1$. The two indicated substitutions transform (22) into

$$\sum_{n=n^*+1}^{\infty}\binom{n}{k}(1-p)^{n-k}=\sum_{j=0}^{k}\binom{n^*+1}{j}p^{j-k-1}(1-p)^{m-j}$$

for $|p|<1$. Multiply both sides by p^{k+1} to get

$$f_R(n^*)=\sum_{n=n^*+1}^{\infty}f(n,k)=\sum_{n=n^*+1}^{\infty}\binom{n}{k}p^{k+1}(1-p)^{n-k}$$

$$=\sum_{j=0}^{k}\binom{n^*+1}{j}p^{j}(1-p)^{m-j}$$

for $|p|<1$ and therefore for $0<p<1$ in particular. This is what we to show in **Exercise 11**.

12. a) Replacing n by $n+1$, $n+2$, $\ldots$, $n+m-1$, we get

$$f(n+1,k)=(1-p)\frac{n+1}{n-k+1}f(n,k)$$

$$\frac{f(n+2,k)}{f(n+1,k)}=(1-p)\frac{n+2}{n-k+2}$$

$$\frac{f(n+3,k)}{f(n+2,k)}=(1-p)\frac{n+3}{n-k+3}$$

$$\cdots$$

$$\frac{f(n+m,k)}{f(n+m-1,k)}=(1-p)\frac{n+m}{n-k+m}.$$

Multiplying these m equations together yields the equation to be proved. The inequality to be proved then follows from

$$\frac{n+1}{n-k+1}>\frac{n+2}{n-k+2}>\cdots>\frac{n+m}{n-k+m}.$$

b) Since $p>K/(N+1)$, we have

$$1-p<1-\frac{K}{N+1}=\frac{N-K+1}{N+1}.$$

Table 4.

Solution to Exercise 12d.

n^*	$\dfrac{f(n^*,4)}{1-R}$
50	2.162×10^{-3}
75	7.674×10^{-6}
100	1.772×10^{-8}
150	4.947×10^{-14}
200	8.747×10^{-20}
250	1.201×10^{-25}

Therefore, we have

$$|R| = R = (1-p)\frac{N+1}{N-K+1} < 1,$$

and the geometric series $\sum_{m=0}^{\infty} f(N,K)R^m$ has sum $f(N,K)/(1-R)$. By part **a**, its terms are larger than those of the positive-term series $\sum_{n=N}^{\infty} f(n,K)$; so we may conclude from the comparison test that the latter series converges, with sum less than $f(N,K)/(1-R)$.

c)

$$\sum_{n=301}^{\infty} f(n,4) < \sum_{m=0}^{\infty} f(301,4) \cdot 0.77^m = \frac{\binom{301}{4}0.25^5 \cdot 0.75^{297}}{0.23}$$

$$< 1.11 \times 10^{-31}.$$

d) We have

$$\frac{f(n^*,4)}{1-R} = \frac{\binom{n^*}{4}0.25^5 \cdot 0.75^{n^*-4}}{1-0.75\left(1+\frac{4}{n^*-3}\right)}.$$

See **Table 4** for the values.

13. See **Figure 4**.

```
2000 REM * This program is in GW-BASIC.
2110 CLS
2120 INPUT "p = ";P
2130 INPUT "k = ";K
2140 INPUT "n* = ";NO
2150 PRINT
2160 REM
3000 REM * Compute fR(n*) by formula (10) applied naively as in
the second
3101 REM * column of Table 2.
3110 LET FR = 1 :  LET K5 = K
3120 FOR N5 = K TO NO
3130     GOSUB 7000
3140     LET FR = FR - F5
3150 NEXT N5
3160 PRINT "Answer to 13a):          ";FR
3170 REM
4000 REM * Compute fr(n*) by method 1.  *
4110 LET FR = 0 :  LET K5 = K
4120 FOR N5 = NO + 1 TO 300
4130     GOSUB 7000
4140     LET FR = FR + F5
4150 NEXT N5
4160 PRINT "Answer to 13b):          ";FR
4170 REM
5000 REM * Compute fr(n*) by formula (11).  *
5110 LET FR = 0 :  LET K5 = NO + 1
5120 FOR K5 = 0 TO K
5130     GOSUB 7000
5140     LET FR = FR + F5/P
5150 NEXT K5
5160 PRINT "Answer to 13c):          ";FR
5170 STOP
5180 REM
7000 REM * Subroutine to compute f(n5,k5,p).  *
7010 REM * Input :  n5, k5, p; Output :  f5 = f(n5,k5,p).  *
7020 LET F5 = P
7030 IF K5 = 0 THEN GOTO 5070
7040 FOR I5 = 1 TO K5
7050     LET F5 = F5 * (N5 - I5 + 1) * P / (K5 - I5 + 1)
7060 NEXT I5
7070 LET F5 = F5 * ((1 - P)^ (N5 - K5))
5080 RETURN
```

Figure 4. A solution to **Exercise 13**.

References

Bespaloff, A. 1980. *The New Signet Book of Wine*, pp. 216–221. New York: New American Library.

A more recent edition was not edited by Bespaloff and unfortunately does not include his interesting description of the solera method.

Cheny, W., and D. Kincaid. 1980. *Numerical Mathematics and Computing*, pp. 27–38. Monterey, CA: Brooks/Cole.

Thoroughly covers the floating-point number system, discusses the hazards of floating-point computation, and offers suggestions on how to reduce the loss of significance that can occur in such computation.

Feller, W. 1967. *An Introduction to Probability Theory and Its Applications*, 3rd ed., pp. 164–167. New York: Wiley.

Considers the "distribution" $f(n, k, p) = \binom{n}{k} p^{k+1} (1 - p)^{n-k}$ in the context of another application, that of waiting times for Bernoulli trials. Feller's approach is somewhat different from ours in that he makes use of *generalized* binomial coefficients

$$\binom{a}{b} = a(a - 1)(a - 2) \ldots (a - b + 1)/b!$$

in which only b is required to be a nonnegative integer.

About the Authors

John T. MacQueen received his Ph.D. in physical chemistry from the University of North Carolina in Chapel Hill in 1962. He has taught at Davidson College, UNC—CH, the College of William and Mary, and Georgetown University. His interests have included general, analytical, and physical chemistry, particularly thermodynamics and statistical mechanics. He has publications on analytical chemistry and the thermodynamics of liquid mixtures. His interest in the solera problem arose while working as a wine merchant.

Rhodes Peele is a member of the mathematics faculty at Auburn University at Montgomery. He taught previously at the University of South Alabama and at Pembroke State University. His 1978 Ph.D. dissertation, also from UNC—CH, concerned matroid theory, a subdiscipline of discrete mathematics, and was directed by Prof. Tom Brylawski. Prof. Peele's research interests and publications concern partition representations of lattices and combinatorial enumeration. He hopes that this article will be a stimulant to improved calculus instruction.

UMAP

Modules in
Undergraduate
Mathematics
and its
Applications

Published in
cooperation with
the Society for
Industrial and
Applied
Mathematics, the
Mathematical
Association of
America, the
National Council of
Teachers of
Mathematics, the
American
Mathematical
Association of Two-
Year Colleges, The
Institute of
Management
Sciences, and the
American Statistical
Association.

Module 705

Information Theory and Biological Diversity

Steven Kolmes
Kevin Mitchell

**Applications of Calculus
to Biology and Ecology**

COMAP, Inc. 60 Lowell Street, Arlington, MA (617) 641-2600

INTERMODULAR DESCRIPTION SHEET:	UMAP Unit 705
TITLE:	Information Theory and Biological Diversity
AUTHOR:	Steven Kolmes Department of Biology and Kevin Mitchell Department of Mathematics and Computer Science Hobart and William Smith Colleges Geneva, NY 14456
MATHEMATICAL FIELD:	Calculus
APPLICATION FIELD:	Biology, ecology
TARGET AUDIENCE:	Students in first- or second-semester calculus course or in a biological modeling course.
ABSTRACT:	Discusses and derives the key properties of one measure of diversity, the entropy function, and illustrates its use by ecologists and animal behaviorists.
PREREQUISITES:	1. Familiarity with the Mean Value Theorem. 2. Familiarity with logarithms and their derivatives. 3. Ability to use the first and second derivatives as aids in graphing functions. 4. L'Hôpital's rule (used once).
OUTPUT SKILLS:	1. Familiarity with one common measure of diversity: $-\sum_{i=1}^{n} p_i \log_2 p_i$. 2. Know how to apply this measure to ecological problems. 3. Greater appreciation of the Mean Value Theorem.
SUGGESTED ADDITIONAL RESOURCE:	Scientific calculator.

©Copyright 1991 by COMAP, Inc. All rights reserved.

COMAP, Inc., 60 Lowell St., Arlington, MA 02174 (617) 641–2600

Information Theory and Biological Diversity

Steven Kolmes
Department of Biology

Kevin Mitchell
Department of Mathematics and Computer Science
Hobart and William Smith Colleges
Geneva, NY 14456

Table of Contents

MODULES AND MONOGRAPHS IN UNDERGRADUATE
MATHEMATICS AND ITS APPLICATIONS (UMAP) PROJECT

The goal of UMAP is to develop, through a community of users and developers, a system of instructional modules in undergraduate mathematics and its applications to be used to supplement existing courses and from which complete courses may eventually be built.

The Project was guided by a National Advisory Board of mathematicians, scientists, and educators. UMAP was funded by a grant from the National Science Foundation and is now supported by the Consortium for Mathematics and Its Applications (COMAP), Inc., a non-profit corporation engaged in research and development in mathematics education.

COMAP Staff

Paul J. Campbell	Editor
Solomon Garfunkel	Executive Director, COMAP
Laurie W. Aragon	Development Director
Philip A. McGaw	Production Manager
Roland Cheyney	Project Manager
Laurie M. Holbrook	Copy Editor
Robin Altomonte	Administrative Asst./Distribution
Dale Horn	Design Assistant

1.   Introduction

This module is concerned with making the notion of "diversity" precise. In commonplace usage, the term is synonomous with "variety" and is simply an indication of the number of different things that are present. For example, we often speak of a "diversity of opinions." While simply counting the number of different types of opinions on a subject can give a rough idea of the "diversity of opinions," the numbers of people holding the various opinions must be taken into account to get a true sense of the diversity. For example, a situation in which there are 99 people with one opinion and 1 person holding a different opinion is different from a situation in which 50 people have one opinion and the other 50 have another, even though the number of opinions (2) is the same in both cases.

Biologists use a mathematical concept called *information* to make precise calculations about entities that we will come to know as *first-order diversity*, H_1, and *divergence from equiprobability*, D_1. We will explore how information theory operates and examine several biological applications of these concepts. In particular, these mathematical entities have proven to be quite useful to ecologists and animal behaviorists. This single set of mathematical formulations, originally intended for use in designing communications systems, has an unusually broad range of applications.

2.   Building Intuition

The following example illuminates the properties that any measure of diversity should have. Assume that you have planted a garden with four types of flowers in equal numbers. Over the course of a growing season, you return to the garden several times to chart the progress of the plants.

In early May, you observe that all of the first three types of flowers have begun to grow. However, only a few of the fourth type of flower are growing. You carefully chart the number of flowers of each flower type as a proportion of the total number of flowers in the garden. Data describing the diversity of plants present would look like **Table 1**.

Table 1.

The garden in May: very few plants of type 4 present.

Flower Type	1	2	3	4
Proportion	5/16	5/16	5/16	1/16

In June, you find that all of the type 4 plants have now sprouted. Each of the four types of plants is now present in equal numbers in the garden. (A situation in which equal proportions of each category are present is a state of *equiprobability,* though "equiproportionality" might be more accurate.) Data describing the diversity of plants would now look like **Table 2**. Notice that the number of types of plants does not change from May to June. However, in May the first three types of flowers dominated the garden, and the fourth type was barely present. By June, all four types of plants are present in equal numbers; none is dominant. Because of this, the diversity of the flower garden increased from May to June.

Table 2.

The garden in June: equiprobability.

Flower Type	1	2	3	4
Proportion	1/4	1/4	1/4	1/4

By August the heat of summer has caused all the flowers of type 2 and half of those of types 1 and 3 to wither and die, though all of the flowers of type 4 are still alive (**Table 3**). The diversity in the garden has decreased from June, because the number of types of flowers present has decreased and one type of flower dominates the garden. It is even less diverse than in May, when three types of flowers were present in equal numbers and a fourth type was present in low numbers.

To assure yourself that the garden in August is less diverse than in May, imagine trying to guess which type of flower you would encounter next in a walk through the garden. In August there is one very common type. By always guessing "type 4" you would be right on average half the time. In May there were three equally common flower types and an additional rare type. Guessing that your next encounter would be with one of the more common types of flower would on average lead to success only five-sixteenths of the time. The greater the diversity of the system, the harder it is to predict what will be encountered next.

Table 3.

The garden in August: low diversity.

Flower Type	1	2	3	4
Proportion	1/4	0	1/4	1/2

By late September, flower types 1 and 3 are now gone because of an early frost; only flower type 4 remains (**Table 4**). The garden is not only less diverse than in August, the garden has no diversity of plant life at all. Every plant is of a single type.

Table 4.

The garden in September: no diversity at all.

Flower Type	1	2	3	4
Proportion	0	0	0	1

What are we to make of this example? Any method we propose to measure diversity needs to reflect the observations that we have just made. Both the number of categories present and the proportions in each category contribute to the overall diversity. The comparison of the May and June gardens indicates that diversity should be maximized when all categories are present in equal proportions and no single category predominates. Secondly, when a system is in such a state of equiprobability, the more categories the system has, the more diverse it will be. (A garden with eight types of flowers present in equal proportions should be more diverse than the June garden with only four types present in equal proportions.) Finally, when all the items fall into a single category, as in the September garden, the measure of diversity should be 0. To summarize, any measure of diversity should satisfy the following three conditions.

Condition 1. *The measure of diversity should be 0 when one of the categories has proportional representation 1 and the rest are represented at a proportion of 0 (not seen).*

Condition 2. *If there are n possible categories, the diversity measure should be maximized when all categories are observed equally, that is, $p_1 = p_2 = \cdots = p_n = \frac{1}{n}$, where p_i is the proportion of the ith category.*

Condition 3. *If $m > n$, then a state of equiprobability (every category observed equally) for a system with m categories should have a higher diversity than a state of equiprobability for a system with only n possible categories.*

3. Diversity Defined

3.1 Proportions

The biological applications discussed in this module are based on reports of field observations. Typically such data are given as an array of proportions of times that particular types of observations were made, much like the data in **Tables 1–4**. Each of the experiments reported will have only a finite number of categories of objects.

Suppose that in a particular experiment exactly n distinct categories were observed, $e_1, e_2, \ldots, e_n$, and that the respective proportions of time they

3

were observed were p_1, p_2, ..., p_n. Then these proportions must satisfy two basic properties.

Property 1. *Each of the numbers p_1, p_2, ..., p_n lies between 0 and 1.*

A proportion of 1 means that all of the observations belong to a single category. A proportion of 0 indicates that no objects belong to that category. (Such a category might still be included in the list if it occurred in some other phase of the experiment.)

Property 2. $\sum_{i=1}^{n} p_i = p_1 + p_2 + \cdots + p_n = 1.$

Property 2 says that the list of events is complete; the proportions of the events e_1, e_2, ..., e_n must sum to 100% of the observations. Notice that the data in **Tables 1–4** satisfy both of these elementary properties.

3.2   The Measure of Diversity

The proportions of different categories of objects in the environment clearly play a role in our intuitive notion of diversity, as illustrated in the garden example above. In that example we were able to rank the relative diversities of the gardens in each month. The June garden had the highest diversity, then May, August, and finally September. However, such a ranking does not permit us to quantify the differences in diversity among the gardens. And such a ranking might be difficult to form when there were 10, 20, or even hundreds of different species of flowers.

How do we make all of this precise? Mathematicians have found a function that satisfies the three conditions listed in Section 2 and also satisfies a number of other important conditions.

Definition 1. *Assume that there are n possible categories in an experiment and that their proportions are p_1, ..., p_n. Then the measure of diversity[1] for this system is*

$$H_1 = -\sum_{i=1}^{n} p_i \log_2 p_i = -(p_1 \log_2 p_1 + p_2 \log_2 p_2 + \cdots + p_n \log_2 p_n).$$

The units of measurement are called *bits*. (Since $\log_2 0$ is not defined, if $p_i = 0$ we adopt the convention that the expression $p_i \log_2 p_i = 0 \log_2 0$ is also 0.)

At this point you probably feel uncertain about the function H_1. As strange as it looks at first glance, this function has become extraordinarily useful not only in mathematics and engineering (especially communications), but also in many of the natural and social sciences. It is worth struggling with because it represents a relatively simple way of quantifying the extremely abstract concept of diversity.

---

[1]In other contexts, this function is also known as the *measure of uncertainty*, *measure of disorder*, or the *entropy* of the system.

3.3 Playing with H_1

To become comfortable with this measure of diversity, we will work out various examples. Let us start by evaluating the different levels of diversity for the flower garden example in Section 2 in each of the four months. In each month there were four possible categories, whose proportions were listed in **Tables 1–4**.

At the first stage, in May (**Table 1**), we have

$$
\begin{aligned}
H_1 &= -\sum_{i=1}^{4} p_i \log_2 p_i \\
&= -\left(\tfrac{5}{16} \log_2 \tfrac{5}{16} + \tfrac{5}{16} \log_2 \tfrac{5}{16} + \tfrac{5}{16} \log_2 \tfrac{5}{16} + \tfrac{1}{16} \log_2 \tfrac{1}{16} \right) \\
&= -\tfrac{15}{16} \log_2 \tfrac{5}{16} - \tfrac{1}{16} \log_2 \tfrac{1}{16} \\
&= \tfrac{15}{16} \log_2 \tfrac{16}{5} + \tfrac{1}{16} \log_2 16 \\
&\approx 1.823 .
\end{aligned}
$$

In June (**Table 2**) we have equiprobability, so

$$
\begin{aligned}
H_1 &= -\sum_{i=1}^{4} p_i \log_2 p_i \\
&= -\left(\tfrac{1}{4} \log_2 \tfrac{1}{4} + \tfrac{1}{4} \log_2 \tfrac{1}{4} + \tfrac{1}{4} \log_2 \tfrac{1}{4} + \tfrac{1}{4} \log_2 \tfrac{1}{4} \right) \\
&= -4 \left(\tfrac{1}{4} \log_2 \tfrac{1}{4} \right) \\
&= -\log_2 \tfrac{1}{4} \\
&= \log_2 4 \\
&= 2 .
\end{aligned}
$$

Notice that the diversity has increased from May to June, as we expected.

With fewer categories present in August (**Table 3**), the diversity is reduced to

$$
\begin{aligned}
H_1 &= -\sum_{i=1}^{4} p_i \log_2 p_i \\
&= -\left(\tfrac{1}{4} \log_2 \tfrac{1}{4} + 0 \log_2 0 + \tfrac{1}{4} \log_2 \tfrac{1}{4} + \tfrac{1}{2} \log_2 \tfrac{1}{2} \right) \\
&= -\tfrac{1}{2} \log_2 \tfrac{1}{4} - \tfrac{1}{2} \log_2 \tfrac{1}{2} \\
&= \tfrac{1}{2} \log_2 4 + \tfrac{1}{2} \log_2 2 \\
&= 1.5 .
\end{aligned}
$$

The diversity in August is lower than in both May and June, and the difference between May and August is larger than the difference between May and June. This reflects the reduction in the number of flower types present in August, as well as the higher proportion of flower type 4.

THE LIBRARY
U.A.M. DRAWER 3599
MONTICELLO, ARKANSAS 716

In September (**Table 4**), as we know, there is no diversity in the garden. Indeed,

$$H_1 = -\sum_{i=1}^{4} p_i \log_2 p_i$$
$$= -(0 \log_2 0 + 0 \log_2 0 + 0 \log_2 0 + 1 \log_2 1)$$
$$= -\log_2 1$$
$$= 0.$$

In fact, in a completely analogous fashion, H_1 will *always* be 0 whenever one of the proportions is 1 and the rest are 0, since $\log_2 1 = 0$. That is, whenever there is complete certainty as to the outcome, $H_1 = 0$. Thus H_1 satisfies the first condition we placed on a measure of diversity, at the end of Section 2.

There are other general observations we can make. Even though the formula for H_1 has a negative sign, H_1 is always nonnegative, because each proportion p_i is between 0 and 1, so that $\log_2 p_i$ is negative or zero.

Next, H_1 is easy to compute in a case of equiprobability. Suppose that there are n equiprobable outcomes. Then for $i = 1, \ldots, n$ we have $p_i = \frac{1}{n}$, so

$$H_1 = -\sum_{i=1}^{n} \frac{1}{n} \log_2 \frac{1}{n} = -n \left(\frac{1}{n} \log_2 \frac{1}{n} \right) = -\log_2 \frac{1}{n} = \log_2 n. \tag{1}$$

We saw an instance of this in the example of the June garden, for which $H_1 = \log_2 4$.

3.4   Computing Base 2 Logarithms

Measures in information theory conventionally use base-2 logarithms; and because most of the data collected in this fashion have used base-2 logarithms, it is probably wise to continue to do so. Mathematically, any base would work. Base-2 logarithms were chosen early on because the original application of information theory was to problems in communication engineering which dealt with binary data (bits, each 0 or 1).

Most calculators allow you to compute the logarithm to base 10 or the natural logarithm (which uses a base of $e = 2.71828\ldots$) of a positive number. Computing the logarithm to base 2 of a positive number is not difficult with a calculator, but it cannot be done with a single keystroke. We need to use the following standard identity:

$$\log_a p = \frac{\log_b p}{\log_b a}. \tag{2}$$

Letting $a = 2$ and $b = 10$, we have

$$\log_2 p = \frac{\log_{10} p}{\log_{10} 2}.$$

For example, with your calculator you can easily check that

$$\log_2 3 = \frac{\log_{10} 3}{\log_{10} 2} \approx 1.585 \,.$$

If you prefer to use natural logarithms, let $b = e$ in **(2)**, so that

$$\log_2 b = \frac{\ln b}{\ln 2} \,.$$

Again with a calculator, you can check that

$$\log_2 3 = \frac{\ln 3}{\ln 2} \approx 1.585 \,.$$

Exercise

1. Use H_1 to calculate the difference in the levels of diversity represented by a garden with 9 types of equally abundant flowers versus a garden with only 5 types of flowers in equal abundance.

3.5   The Divergence from Equiprobability

Definition 2. *In an experiment with n categories, $H_{1max}(n)$ is the maximum possible value of H_1.*

(When the number of categories is understood from the context, this quantity will be denoted by H_{1max}.)

In Section 4 we will show that such a maximum always exists and in fact occurs when all n categories are equiprobable, so that H_1 satisfies the second condition of a diversity measure. Showing that H_1 satisfies the third condition of a diversity measure is left as an exercise.

The maximum value for H_1 provides a way to measure how far from equiprobability a particular set of proportions is.

Definition 3. *The divergence from equiprobability is*

$$D_1 = H_{1max} - H_1 = \log_2 n - H_1,$$

where n is the number of categories in the system.

A low D_1 value means H_1 is close to H_{1max}, that is, the system is nearly in a state of equiprobability; there is a high degree of diversity present. Conversely, a high D_1 value means that H_1 is small relative to H_{1max}, that is, the system has diverged substantially from equiprobability and is not very diverse.

For example, in the August garden, only three of the four flower types were present (**Table 3**). The H_1 value for the system was calculated to be 1.5. Thus the divergence from equiprobability in this case is

$$D_1 = H_{1max} - H_1 = (\log_2 4) - 1.5 = 2.0 - 1.5 = 0.5 \,.$$

This is a substantial divergence, since it represents 25% of H_{1max}.

Exercises

2. Use **(1)** to show that H_1 satisfies the third condition in Section 2 for a diversity measure by comparing H_1 in two different equiprobability situations: one with m outcomes and the other with n.

3. **Table 5** shows the distribution of MN blood groups in a population of Bedouins in the Syrian desert. Calculate the diversity, H_1, and the divergence, D_1, for this data set.

Table 5.

Distribution of Blood Groups in Bedouins
(adapted from [Boyd 1939, 234]).

Blood Group	MM	MN	NN
Proportion	0.57	0.37	0.06

4. **Table 6** shows the distribution of the ABO blood groups in four different populations.

Table 6.

Distribution of ABO Blood Groups
(adapted from [Boyd 1950, 223-225]).

Population	A	B	AB	O
Germans	0.425	0.145	0.065	0.365
Basques	0.417	0.011	0.000	0.572
Navajos	0.225	0.000	0.000	0.775
Chinese	0.251	0.342	0.100	0.307

a) Using H_1 calculations, determine which population has the most diverse distribution of blood groups, and which population has the least.

b) Determine the divergence D_1 for each of the populations.

5. In **Exercises 3** and **4**, field data are reported as arrays of proportions of times observations were made. This makes doing H_1 calculations quite easy. However, often such data are given as an array of raw frequencies of observations, as in **Table 7**.

  Calculations of H_1 can be made directly from raw frequency data, without ever converting to proportions, if rules for logarithms are used. Let

Table 7.
Distribution of ABO Blood Groups
(adapted from [Boyd 1950, 223-225]).

Population	O	A	B	AB	Total
Siamese	79	38	75	21	213
English	202	179	35	6	422
Blackfeet Indian	27	88	0	0	115

$f_1, \ldots, f_n$ represent the observed frequencies of the n events $e_1, \ldots, e_n$. Let S denote the total number of observations,

$$S = \sum_{i=1}^{n} f_i = f_1 + \cdots + f_n.$$

Then the proportion of time event e_i was observed is $p_i = f_i/S$.

a) Use this expression for p_i to show that

$$H_1 = \log_2 S - \frac{1}{S} \sum_{i=1}^{n} f_i \log_2 f_i.$$

b) **Table 7** shows the distribution of ABO blood groups in three populations. Compute the measure of diversity of blood types for each of the three populations by using the formula you derived in **(a)**.

c) Which of the three groups has the highest divergence of blood types?

4. The Proof that $H_{1\max} = \log_2 n$

4.1 Properties of $x \log_2 x$

Let us suppose now that there are n possible categories in a particular experiment, with $n > 1$. The calculation of H_1 involves summing quantities of the general form $x \log_2 x$, with x taking on each of the values p_1 through p_n, with p_i representing the proportion of observations from the ith category. To show that $H_{1\max}$ occurs when $p_1 = p_2 = \cdots = p_n = \frac{1}{n}$, we will use elementary calculus to describe certain properties of the function $x \log_2 x$.

We begin by formalizing our convention that $x \log_2 x = 0$ when $x = 0$. We define a new function F whose domain is $0 \leq x \leq 1$:

$$F(x) = \begin{cases} 0, & \text{if } x = 0; \\ x \log_2 x, & \text{if } 0 < x \leq 1. \end{cases}$$

To make differentiation of $F(x)$ an easier task, we will employ the fact that

$$\log_2 x = \frac{\ln x}{\ln 2}.$$

If we agree to let $k = 1/\ln 2$, then we can write:

$$F(x) = \begin{cases} 0, & \text{if } x = 0; \\ kx \ln x, & \text{if } 0 < x \le 1. \end{cases}$$

Observe that $F(x)$ is continuous for $0 < x \le 1$, because both x and $\ln x$ are continuous. To see what happens at 0, we argue as follows:

$$\lim_{x \to 0^+} F(x) = \lim_{x \to 0^+} kx \ln x = \lim_{x \to 0^+} \frac{k \ln x}{1/x}.$$

Now employ l'Hôpital's Rule:

$$\lim_{x \to 0^+} \frac{k \ln x}{1/x} = \lim_{x \to 0^+} \frac{k/x}{-1/x^2} = \lim_{x \to 0^+} -kx = 0 = F(0).$$

That is, we have shown that $\lim_{x \to 0^+} F(x) = F(0)$, so F is continuous on the closed interval $[0, 1]$.

Finally, observe that for $0 < x < 1$, the first two derivatives of F are:

$$
\begin{align}
F'(x) &= k + k \ln x, & \text{(3)} \\
F''(x) &= k/x. & \text{(4)}
\end{align}
$$

In particular, notice that since k is positive, $F''(x) > 0$. Consequently, $F'(x)$ is increasing and $F(x)$ is convex (concave up).

Exercise

6. Graph the function F and mark any extreme points.

4.2   Using the Mean Value Theorem

The convexity of $F(x)$ turns out to be the crucial fact in determining $H_{1\max}$. To see this, recall the following result from differential calculus.

Mean Value Theorem. *If a function f is continuous on the closed interval $[a, b]$ and differentiable on the open interval (a, b), then there exists at least one number c in (a, b) such that*

$$f'(c) = \frac{f(b) - f(a)}{b - a}.$$

Geometrically, the Mean Value Theorem means that the slope of the secant line over the entire interval is the same as the slope of the tangent line at some intermediate point in the interval (**Figure 1**).

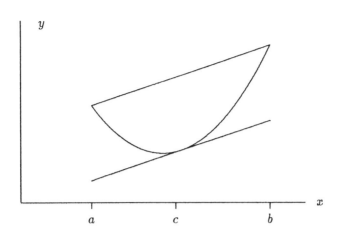

Figure 1. The Mean Value Theorem. The slope of the secant over $[a, b]$ is the same as the slope of the tangent at some intermediate point c in the interval.

Corollary 1. *Assume f is a continuous function on the closed interval $[a, b]$, differentiable on (a, b), and that f' is an increasing function. For $a \leq r < t < v \leq b$, we have*

$$\frac{f(t) - f(r)}{t - r} \leq f'(t) \leq \frac{f(v) - f(t)}{v - t}. \tag{5}$$

Proof: The Mean Value Theorem applies to f on both of the intervals $[r, t]$ and $[t, v]$. Consequently, there exist points s and u in (r, t) and (t, v), respectively, such that

$$f'(s) = \frac{f(t) - f(r)}{t - r} \quad \text{and} \quad f'(u) = \frac{f(v) - f(t)}{v - t}.$$

Since $s < t < u$ and f' is by hypothesis an increasing function, we have

$$f'(s) \leq f'(t) \leq f'(u)$$

and the result follows.

The geometric meaning of **Corollary 1** (see **Figure 2**) is that if f is a differentiable convex function, then the slopes of two successive secants to the curve are increasing, and the slope of the tangent at their intersection is intermediate to the slopes.

Corollary 2. *Assume f is continuous on the closed interval $[a, b]$, differentiable on (a, b), and that f' is an increasing function. Let t be any point in (a, b). Then for any point p in $[a, b]$,*

$$f(p) \geq f(t) + f'(t)(p - t). \tag{6}$$

11

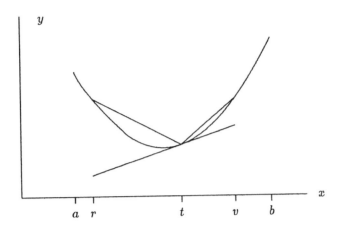

Figure 2. $f'(t)$ is intermediate to the slope of successive secants.

Proof: There are three possibilities: $p = t$, $p < t$, or $p > t$. In the case $p = t$, **(6)** reduces to the trivial assertion that $f(t) \geq f(t)$.

Now assume that $p < t$. Using p for r in the first half of **(5)**,

$$\frac{f(t) - f(p)}{t - p} \leq f'(t).$$

Consequently we have

$$f(t) - f(p) \leq f'(t)(t - p),$$

so

$$-f(p) \leq -f(t) + f'(t)(t - p).$$

Since $t - p = -(p - t)$, by multiplying this last inequality by -1, we obtain the desired result:

$$f(p) \geq f(t) + f'(t)(p - t).$$

The case $p > t$ is similar and is left as an exercise.

Corollary 2 has a simple geometric interpretation. Let f be a differentiable convex curve. Recall that the tangent line to f at t is given by

$$y - f(t) = f'(t)(x - t).$$

In particular, when $x = p$, we find

$$y = f(t) + f'(t)(p - t).$$

But **Corollary 2** says that for any point p,

$$f(p) \geq f(t) + f'(t)(p - t).$$

That is, the graph of a differentiable convex function lies above any of its tangent lines, as can be seen in either **Figure 1** or **2**.

Exercise

7. Do the case $p > t$ in the proof of **Corollary 2**.

4.3   Convexity and $H_{1\max}$

Now we can complete the proof that $H_{1\max} = \log_2 n$ for systems with n possible states. It follows from **(3)** and **(4)** in Section 4.1 that the function

$$F(x) = \begin{cases} 0, & \text{if } x = 0; \\ kx \ln x, & \text{if } 0 < x \leq 1 \end{cases}$$

satisfies the conditions of **Corollary 2** on the closed interval $[0,1]$. Let $t = \frac{1}{n}$; then for any proportion p_i, **Corollary 2** implies

$$F(p_i) \geq F(\tfrac{1}{n}) + F'(\tfrac{1}{n})\left(p_i - \tfrac{1}{n}\right).$$

Summing this inequality over all n probabilities for the system, we obtain

$$
\begin{aligned}
\sum_{i=1}^{n} p_i \log_2 p_i &= \sum_{i=1}^{n} F(p_i) \\
&\geq \sum_{i=1}^{n} \left(F(\tfrac{1}{n}) + F'(\tfrac{1}{n})(p_i - \tfrac{1}{n}) \right) \\
&= \sum_{i=1}^{n} F(\tfrac{1}{n}) + \sum_{i=1}^{n} F'(\tfrac{1}{n})(p_i - \tfrac{1}{n}) \\
&= nF(\tfrac{1}{n}) + F'(\tfrac{1}{n}) \left(\sum_{i=1}^{n} p_i - \sum_{i=1}^{n} \tfrac{1}{n} \right) \\
&= nF(\tfrac{1}{n}) + F'(\tfrac{1}{n})(1 - 1) \\
&= nF(\tfrac{1}{n}).
\end{aligned}
$$

That is,

$$\sum_{i=1}^{n} p_i \log_2 p_i \geq nF(\tfrac{1}{n}),$$

so

$$-\sum_{i=1}^{n} p_i \log_2 p_i \leq -nF(\tfrac{1}{n}),$$

and hence

$$H_1 \leq -n \left(\tfrac{1}{n} \log_2 \tfrac{1}{n} \right) = \log_2 n,$$

which fact completes the proof and shows that H_1 satisfies **Condition 2** of a diversity measure in Section 2.

5.   Information Theory Applications

5.1   Three Applications to Ecological Diversity

The most common biological application of information theory is quantification of ecological diversity. When an ecosystem possesses numerous plant and animal species, with many of them present in relatively high numbers, it will have a high H_1 value and a low D_1. An ecosystem with fewer types of organisms present, or with only a few common plant or animal species, will concomitantly have lower H_1 and higher D_1 values.

We generally think of healthy biological communities in favorable habitats as being highly diverse. Decreased biological diversity may be due to environmental conditions (desert versus a temperate zone forest) or to stresses on a biological community (acid rain or pesticides), which eliminate susceptible species from the natural mix. Information theory allows us to quantify both stress-induced and natural differences between ecosystems.

Even natural changes in the the diversity of an ecosystem can be quite dramatic. Twice in the last twenty years, there have been major infestations of the crown of thorns starfish, *Acanthaster planci*, on the Great Barrier Reef. The crown of thorns attacks certain species of corals that build and maintain the reef. In some areas as much as 98% of the coral is dead, though it is not clear whether the crown of thorns is responsible for all of this destruction. Initially marine ecologists in Australia were alarmed by these infestations. However, opinion is now beginning to shift.

> Not only do some experts think the coral can recover from the crown of thorns. Some marine scientists also think it might be good for the reef to go through such growing pains. Their argument is essentially that the crown of thorns, like a renovator, may make a terrible mess on the way toward home improvements in the longer term. In particular, the crown of thorns cuts down the dominant species of coral and thus makes room for other species, currently crowded out, the upshot being a more diverse group of corals. Biologists have known for a long time that the starfish in temperate waters, by eating common things like mussels, clear out space for other species, and the same kind of benefits, they argue, may accrue from the "destruction" caused by the crown of thorns. [Ford 1988, 51]

Changes in the diversity of an ecosystem are important, as the example above indicates. Ecologists call the first-order diversity of an ecosystem the *Shannon index* [Lloyd, Zar, and Karr 1968]. An H_1 value can be computed for all of the organisms present in an environment, or for specific types of organisms such as trees or insects. Because the presence of uncommon species in nature can make information theory measures sensitive to the sizes of data sets (in general, only large sets will contain representatives of all the rare

14

species), it is for important for comparisons of biological diversity to collect similar-sized data sets.

5.1.1 Tree Species Diversity

Table 8 contains H_1 values for mature trees found in different types of forests in Florida [Monk 1967]. Habitats of the sandhill complex type have fairly simple mature tree communities ($H_1 = 0.97$) compared to an area of sand pine scrub ($H_1 = 1.55$). The most complex mature tree community is the climax southern mixed hardwoods ($H_1 = 2.56$), into which the other forest types listed change very slowly by a process known as *ecological succession*. Information theory measures do distinguish between these different natural communities.

Table 8

H_1 values for trees in plant communities in Florida (from [Monk 1967, 175]).

Community	H_1 of Mature Trees
Sandhill Complex	0.97
Cypress Heads	1.16
Sand Pine Scrub	1.55
Mixed Hardwood Swamps	2.28
Climax Southern Mixed Hardwoods	2.56

5.1.2 Bird Species Diversity

Ornithologists have noted that more types of birds are present breeding in woodlands than in fields of similar sizes. MacArthur and MacArthur [1961] used first-order diversity measures to investigate the relationship between bird diversity and vegetation. They measured H_1 values for the diversities of bird species breeding at 11 deciduous woodland locations in Pennsylvania, Vermont, and Maryland.

In the same habitats they measured various aspects of the vegetation in order to look for any plant community characteristics that were strongly cor-related with bird species diversities. Plant species diversities were computed by using H_1 values. Foliage height diversities, which expressed the number of layers of leaves between the ground and the sky in different woodlands, were also measured. Zones of 0 to 2 feet, 2 to 25 feet, and greater than 25 feet above the ground were used as height categories. The number of leaves above points on the ground were estimated for each height zone, and H_1 val-ues for the foliage height diversity were then calculated. When the number of leaves above the ground in the three height zones are more nearly equal, the foliage height diversity measure increases to reflect the more complex physical environment.

The simplest model of how birds select a nesting habitat is that as either foliage height diversity or plant species diversity increases, the attractiveness of the habitat increases linearly. MacArthur and MacArthur [1961] looked for such a relationship. Bird species diversity and foliage height diversity were strongly correlated. **Figure 3** shows this correlation as a linear relationship. The data closely approximate the line given by the equation

$$\text{bird species diversity} = 2.01 \times \text{foliage height diversity} + 0.46 \,.$$

On the basis of this linear relationship, birds appear to be selecting nesting habitats on the basis of foliage height diversities.

Interestingly, there was a much weaker relationship between bird species diversity and plant species diversity measures. The plot of bird species diversity versus plant species diversity is considerably less linear than the plot using foliage height diversity. The physical structure of the woodlands, in terms of the leaves present in different height zones, seems to matter more to the birds than the species of plants producing those physical structures.

5.1.3   The Effect of Insecticide Application

Species diversity values can also be used to measure changes in a single habitat over time. **Figure 4** shows the effect of experimental insecticide application on H_1 values for arthropods in a treated grassland compared to an untreated control habitat [Barrett 1968]. The untreated control area (dashed line) does not display the dramatic drop in H_1 values immediately after application of the insecticide sevin (indicated by the shaded time period) that is seen in the treated area (solid line). A similar approach can be used to measure the effects of accidentally released pollutants.

Measurements like the ones discussed for tree species diversity, bird species diversity, and insecticide effects, can be carried out using a number of different diversity index [Pielou 1975, 1984; Magurran 1988].

Exercises

8. Before settlement by Europeans, the Great Lakes Region of the United States was covered by a vast pine forest. Recent studies of this vanished forest area have relied on modern analysis of data collected during the General Land Office survey of Michigan carried out in the 1800s [Whitney 1986]. The data in **Table 9** show the percentage of trees reported as "bearing trees" by surveyors in two different habitats in Northern Michigan, sometime between 1836 and 1859 [Whitney 1986].

   a) Determine the the diversity of the tree species, H_1, for each of the two areas in **Table 9**.

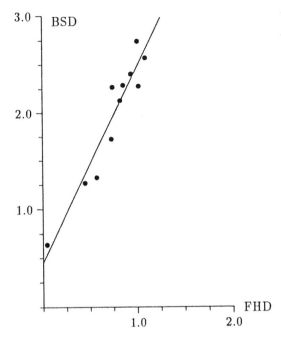

Site	BSD	FHD	PSD
A	0.639	0.043	0.972
B	1.266	0.448	1.911
C	2.265	0.745	2.344
D	2.403	0.943	1.768
E	1.721	0.731	1.372
F	2.739	1.009	2.503
G	1.332	0.577	1.367
H	2.285	0.859	1.776
I	2.277	1.021	2.464
J	2.127	0.825	2.176
K	2.567	1.093	2.816

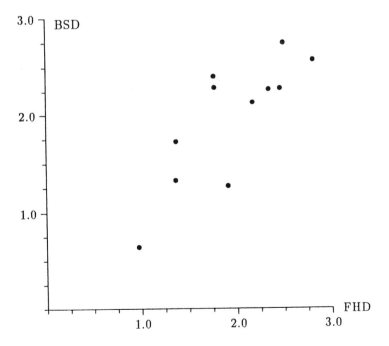

Figure 3. Bird species diversity (BSD) plotted against foliage height diversity (FHD) and against plant species diversity (PSD). Adapted from [MacArthur and MacArthur 1961, 596].

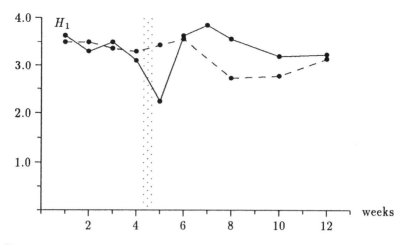

Figure 4. The effect of insecticide application (shaded region) on H_1 values of a treated habitat (solid line) and an untreated control habitat (dashed line). Modified from [Odum 1971, 150].

Table 9.

Percentage of species of trees reported in two forest areas in Michigan. Modified from [Whitney 1986, 1552]).

Species	Swamps	Uplands
Balsam fir	1.7	0.0
Red maple	1.6	2.6
Sugar maple	0.1	3.0
Yellow birch	0.5	0.0
White birch	2.9	0.4
Birch	2.5	0.8
Beech	0.2	17.2
White ash	0.7	0.0
Black ash	3.6	0.0
Tamarack	29.7	0.0
Spruce	10.6	0.0
Pitch pine	1.7	10.9
Norway pine	1.1	25.7
Pine	1.5	7.5
White pine	7.6	12.7
Poplar	3.8	2.2
White oak	0.0	5.7
Black oak	0.0	3.4
Cedar	25.2	0.0
Hemlock	3.2	7.3
Elm	1.0	0.1
Miscellaneous	0.8	0.5

b) Determine the the divergence from equiprobability, D_1, of the tree species for each of the two areas in **Table 9**.

9. Honey bees perform tasks inside the hive when they are newly-emerged workers, and switch to collecting nectar and pollen from flowers later in their lives. Numerous studies of honey bee behavior have revealed that the tasks they perform inside the hive are quite varied and complex. The data in **Table 10** show all of the behavioral patterns recorded for three worker bees that represent a very small part of the group observed in an experiment [Kolmes 1985]. Although three bees is too small a group from which to draw any conclusions, we can still get a sense of the diversity of behavior patterns.

Table 10.

Data for honey bee behavior inside the hive. Modified from [Kolmes 1985].

Behavior	Bee 1	Bee 2	Bee 3
Walk	9	7	8
Stand	7	7	2
Groom Self	4	7	5
Inspect/Feed	1	1	2
Into Empty Cell	2	5	1
Into Honey Cell	0	1	0
Into Pollen Cell	0	1	0
Build Comb	0	3	0
Groom Other Bee	0	0	4
Get Groomed	0	0	1
Get Fed	0	0	1
DVAV	1	0	0
Attend Dance	3	0	0
Antennate	2	2	0
Chew Hive	1	0	0
Fan	1	2	0

a) Determine the the diversity of the behaviors, H_1, for each of the three bees in **Table 10**.

b) Determine the the divergence from equiprobability, D_1, of the behaviors for each of the three bees in **Table 10**.

5.2   Fire Ants

Fire ants of the species *Solenopsis saevissima* are social insects that live in underground nests containing many sterile workers and their queen. To obtain food, workers set forth from the nest and search the surrounding area. If a worker finds a food source large enough for a number of ants to harvest, a communication system based on odor trails allows additional ants to be recruited [Wilson 1962].

To produce an odor trail, a worker returning to the nest periodically drags its sting along the ground while releasing a chemical produced by Dufour's gland through the extruded sting. The chemical released is attractive to other workers and causes them to follow the odor trail towards the food. A truly abundant food source eventually produces a situation in which many ants returning from the food to the nest are excited into producing an odor trail and the summed individual odor trails produces a virtual chemical "highway" leading to the food. The chemical secreted from Dufour's gland fades slowly over time, so that a depleted food source loses its attractiveness.

In the absence of any odor trail, a foraging worker leaving a fire ant nest might be expected to depart without bias towards any particular direction, that is, in any one of the 360° of directions that surround the nest. The diversity of directions that a departing group of ants might be expected to display in this uninformed initial circumstance would be

$$H_i = \log_2 360$$

in which every 1° of direction is taken as a potential direction category.

If there is an odor trail to a food source, then the departing ants might be expected to depart from their nest in a smaller angular range of directions. If the smaller diversity of this range of directions is symbolized by H_s, then the transmission of information by the odor trail, denoted H_t, must equal the difference between the diversity of the array of departure directions displayed by the informed ants and that displayed by the uninformed groups of ants. That is,

$$H_t = H_i - H_s.$$

Using a small drop of sugar solution placed on an index card as a food source, Wilson [1962] measured the direction indicated by the odor trail produced by a single fire ant and its influence upon the directions in which recruited foragers travelled from their nest. After this procedure was carried out a number of times to obtain replicate data sets, an estimate of the information transmitted by fire ant odor trails could be made.[2]

---

[2] H_s can be measured either by observing the distribution of directions by which ants depart from their nest and counting the number of ants in each degree-category, or by considering the data to be a normally distributed one-dimesional Gaussian distribution and applying the formula $H_s = \log_2 \sqrt{2\pi e}\, \sigma$, with σ the standard deviation. See Haldane and Spurway [1954] or Wilson [1962] for more details concerning the latter approach.

The results of the fire ant study showed a considerable amount of information transmission by the odor trails (see **Table 11**). When food sources were placed between 20 mm and 100 mm from an ant nest, the range of directional information transmitted by odor trails proved to be between 3 and 5 bits.

Table 11.

The amount of directional information transmitted to single workers by a single fire ant odor trail (adapted from [Wilson 1962, 152]).

Target range (mm)	H_t
20	2.81
50	4.11
100	5.10

We can interpret one bit of information in this context in the following way. If a foraging ant could only inform another worker that a food source was either to the north or the south of the nest, there would be only two directional choices, so $H_{1max} = H_i = \log_2 2 = 1$. If the communication that took place was perfect and the second worker always went in the correct direction, then $H_s = 1 \log_2 1 = 0$. In this simple situation,

$$H_t = H_i - H_s = 1.$$

Now assume the foraging ant could perfectly transmit the information as to whether the food source was to the north, east, south , or west, then $H_i = \log_2 4 = 2$ bits since there are now four directional categories. In the same manner, we can interpret the 3 to 5 bits of information conveyed by the foraging ants in this experiment. The 3 to 5 bits of information transmitted is equivalent to every departing forager being told what direction to walk and being equipped with a tiny compass upon which are marked between $2^3 = 8$ and $2^5 = 32$ directional points. Departing foragers given such equipment, and able to use it well, would be able to depart in a given direction as accurately as departing ants using an odor trail rather than a tiny compass as their guide [Wilson 1962, 154].

The main reason for converting the actual field data regarding trail communication into abstract "bits of information" is that doing so allows us to compare the very different communication systems employed by a wide range of insects and animals, e.g., the information conveyed by a honey bee's waggle dance vs. that of a fire ant's odor trail.

A foraging honey bee that has located a rich source of nectar and pollen will perform a waggle dance upon its return to its hive. The dance allows the other bees to find the food source. The waggle dance looks rather like a "figure-8" performed on a vertical surface inside the hive. Its interpretation involves both the orientation of the dance and its pace. The direction to a food source is encoded by the angle that the figure-8 deviates from the vertical. The distance to the food source is encoded by the number of turns per minute that a dancing bee performs. Haldane and Spurway [1954] analyzed the information transmitted by dancing bees to other foragers. Honey bees transmit between 2.5 and 4.0 bits of directional information in their waggle dance.

Both honey bees and fire ants are quite good at directing nestmates to food sources, although the methods they use to communicate with each other differ dramatically.

5.3   Information Theory and Fish Courtship

Information theory was used by J. R. Baylis [1976] to quantify communication during the courtship of cichlid fishes. These fishes form pair bonds between male and female. After the female releases her eggs for fertilization by the male, both parents take part in an extended period of parental care. Both the eggs and the young fry that hatch from them are guarded by the parents; and especially when the young have developed into a motile "swarm" of tiny fishes, protecting them from potential predators requires considerable efforts by both parents. Because of this vital joint responsibility, cichlid fishes have an extended period of courtship communication that allows each fish to evaluate in some fashion how good a mate and fellow-guardian its potential partner would be.

Baylis [1976] categorized the behavior patterns of the fish into 10 event categories corresponding to the various body postures and movements that make up the repertoire of courtship signals. Both males and females can carry out any of the 10 categories.

All of the fish used were young animals who were sexually mature but who had never previously spawned, so there were no previously learned aspects of social signalling to influence the behavior of the fish. The male and female fish were then placed together in an aquarium. Baylis periodically watched the fish, from initial introduction until their fry were free swimming.

The data form a preceding act/following act matrix, with 20 rows and 20 columns, with 10 columns for each behavior pattern for the male fish and 10 for the female fish. The 20 rows were labelled similarly. The data in the cells of the matrix are the frequencies with which given behavior patterns (e.g., "male performs behavior pattern number 2") were immediately followed by other behavior patterns (e.g., "female performs behavior pattern number 4"). Since communication consists of a signal and its response, this arrangement records signal–response pairs. By having the sexes on both rows and columns, it was possible to record an animal receiving a reply to its signal (that is, a male responded to by a female, or vice versa) and also an animal "repeating itself" (that is, a male or female sending 2 signals in a row, without an intervening reply from the other fish). If you consider for a moment how frequently humans must repeat questions before being answered, it will be obvious why the matrix was arranged to allow recording of repetition.

Each matrix is for a particular time in the sequence of courtship behavior. The entire set of observations is a set of data matrices, each labelled with the time of recording (e.g., "1 hour after the fish were placed together in the observation aquarium").

An inspection of the matrix in **Table 12** tells us a bit about what is going on. For example, males often followed one "quiver" display with another (row F, column F). Roughly half as often, a female responds with a "quiver" to a male's "quiver" display (row F, column FF). But this approach to analyzing the matrix is a tedious one; what can information theory tell us here?

We can use row and column totals to compute first-order information theory measures. As courtship proceeds, we would expect to see the divergence from equiprobability (D_1) increase for a pair of fish. The signals sent by each sex may begin with a high first-order uncertainty (H_1). However, unless the fish begin to abandon signals unnecessary to spawning and to concentrate on the final spawning signals (therefore reducing H_1 and increasing D_1) they will never produce young together.

In a human analogy, unless their conversation abandons topics such as the weather and television, two people are never going to learn enough about each other to decide whether or not a mutual attraction and set of shared values exists. The divergence from equiprobability of their conversation must increase, that is, they must move beyond initial polite phrases ("Nice day, isn't it?") if anything more involved than "small talk" is to occur eventually.

The first-order measures can be computed by summing the preceding acts (rows) or the following acts (columns) and treating the total values as two one-dimensional 20-category matrices. The quantities H_1, H_{1max}, and D_1 are then computed as in any other example.

Baylis [1976] found for pairs of cichlid fish that the first-order measures (increasing D_1 values) reflected the process of courtship communication. Notice in **Figure 5** the way the first-order measures are clearly structured around the moment of spawning, with D_1 increasing just before spawning. The fish do begin to concentrate on the use of specific signals immediately before the female releases her eggs and the male releases sperm to fertilize them. Animals with external fertilization of this sort must be very well behaviorally synchronized if the male and female are both to release their gametes at the same moment.

The approach to animal communication just demonstrated does not, in the final analysis, allow us to achieve the ultimate goal of "talking to the animals." It does, however, provide one of the best means devised to date of

Table 12. A transition array of preceding (rows) and following (columns) behaviors observed during observation period 1 for three pairs of *Cichlasoma citrinellum*. Adapted from [Baylis 1976, 125].

Preceding Act

Following Act

			Male											Female							
Behavior	A	B	C	D	E	F	G	H	I	J	a	b	c	d	e	f	g	h	i	j
Male																				
A. Bite	1	0	0	0	0	0	0	0	0	0	0	0	0	0	0	0	0	1	0	0
B. Frontal	0	0	6	0	0	2	0	0	0	1	0	5	9	0	1	1	0	5	1	1
C. Lateral	0	0	19	4	76	76	0	1	10	86	0	13	53	11	3	65	1	1	61	122
D. Dig	0	0	2	1	1	0	0	0	0	2	0	1	1	0	0	6	0	0	1	5
E. Tailbeat	1	0	9	0	87	12	0	0	0	21	0	5	6	3	1	7	0	2	16	30
F. Quiver	0	0	22	2	3	184	0	0	26	24	0	1	0	8	0	95	0	0	54	36
G. Skim	0	0	0	0	0	0	0	0	0	0	0	0	0	0	0	0	0	0	0	0
H. Yield	0	0	1	0	0	0	0	0	0	0	0	0	0	0	0	1	0	0	0	0
I. Nip Off	0	0	4	3	1	19	0	0	35	9	0	0	0	0	0	15	0	0	5	27
J. Approach	0	17	73	1	6	9	0	0	5	12	0	4	13	10	0	79	0	8	61	63
Female																				
a. Bite	0	0	0	0	0	0	0	1	0	0	0	0	0	0	0	0	0	0	0	0
b. Frontal	0	7	116	0	2	0	0	0	1	0	0	0	3	0	0	1	0	0	0	3
c. Lateral	0	0	38	0	5	2	0	0	1	7	0	2	5	1	2	8	1	0	6	26
d. Dig	0	0	8	2	1	7	0	0	1	12	0	0	1	12	0	27	0	0	1	14
e. Tailbeat	0	0	3	0	3	0	0	0	0	1	0	0	1	0	6	1	0	0	0	0
f. Quiver	0	0	49	5	3	80	0	0	25	67	0	0	2	27	1	287	1	1	66	65
g. Skim	0	0	0	0	0	0	0	0	0	0	0	0	0	0	0	0	0	0	2	0
h. Yield	0	0	0	0	0	0	0	0	0	0	4	0	0	3	1	0	5	0	0	7
i. Nip Off	0	2	39	10	2	28	0	0	5	87	0	0	1	11	1	56	0	1	317	38
j. Approach	0	6	214	2	2	36	0	0	9	25	1	102	7	1	0	26	0	0	6	16

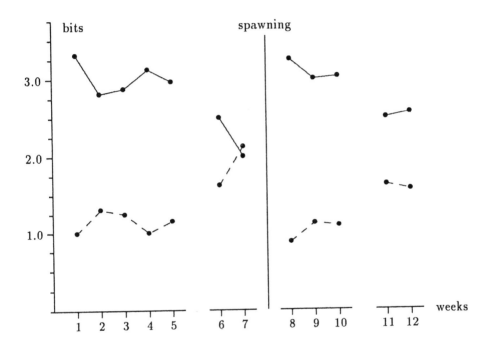

Figure 5. First-order diversity, H_1, (solid line) and divergence from equiprobability, D_1, (dashed line) of courtship during 12 observation periods in three pairs of *Cichlasoma citrinellum*. Adapted from [Baylis 1976, 134].

quantifying animal communication. It is a bit amusing, however, that information theory, with its origins in devising communication systems, allows us to "listen in" (however imperfectly) to "conversations" between members of other species.

Exercises

10. The data in **Table 13** show how responsive different female white-crowned sparrows (*Zonotrichia leucophrys*) were to the recorded courtship songs of male sparrows of two species raised in the laboratory. Responses to their own species are in the top row and responses to a related species (song sparrow) are in the bottom row. Animal communication must follow predictable patterns for it to be effective, so we might expect a more consistent response by female sparrows to appropriate (same species) male songs than to inappropriate (different species) male courtship songs. Information theory measures are one way of addressing how consistently a group of experimental animals responds to different stimuli.

Table 13.

Responses by 13 female white-crowned sparrows to male white-crowned sparrows (W-CS) and male song sparrows (SS). Adapted from [Spitler-Nabors and Baker 1987, 383].

Female	a	b	c	d	e	f	g	h	i	j	k	l	m
W-CS	1	4	10	1	4	20	1	1	1	7	14	1	3
SS	2	0	10	0	0	14	27	0	0	0	10	0	4

a) Determine which of the laboratory-raised male sparrows elicited a more diverse response from the 13 female white-crowned sparrows.

b) What is the divergence for each data set? From just looking at the data, do you expect this divergence to be high or low (as a proportion of H_{1max})?

6. Sample Projects

We have discussed a number of applications of information theory measures. It is your turn to design an independent project in which you will collect data and use information theory measures in your analysis. You may choose to make a local insect collection, to examine the types of insect pollinators that visit various flowers, to measure bird diversity or plant diversity, to examine conversational topics or the types of clothing worn by your fellow students. We encourage you to develop an entirely novel topic. Should the size of your proposed project make it reasonable, a team effort might be appropriate.

You may want to compare two systems, as in Section 5.1.1. Or you might design a project which compares two or more different diversity indices to each other, as in Section 5.1.2. You may even want to compare one system to itself over time, as in Sections 5.1.3 and 5.3. Whatever you select, information theory measures are widely applicable; and with a little imagination you should be able to come up with an interesting topic. Birds, bees, flowers, friends, food—anything that exists in a naturally diverse array is a good place to look for a topic. Below, we outline the procedures for a few sample projects.

Here are a few reminders before you begin. First, the categories you use must not overlap and together must include all possible events. Second, you should have a well-defined sampling procedure (devised beforehand) that you follow to collect your data, to prevent unconscious biases from entering your data set. Third, it may be simpler to do your diversity calculations with raw frequencies (as in **Exercise 5**) rather than converting your data to proportions.

6.1 Diversity of Flowers

Select two or more different areas of open field. Try to select areas that look different in an overall way to you, such as a field of clover and Queen Anne's lace, and a small meadow in the middle of the woods filled with spring ephemeral flowers. If you select areas that differ in a visual and intuitive way, you can go on to see whether or not they differ in a quantifiable fashion. In each area carry out the following procedure.

1. Start on one edge of of the field and begin to walk straight towards some obvious landmark.

2. Every two paces, stop and drop in front of you a 30 cm $\times$ 30 cm square made of pipecleaners.

3. Examine all of the flowers inside the square. Assign each one to a category, and keep track of how many flowers of each type you see. Carrying a

notebook to which you tape a single representative of each of the flower categories can help you keep them straight. If you are artistically inclined, you may wish to make sketches.

4. Note that you do not need to know the names of the flowers. So long as your categories are unambiguous and include all of the types of flowers you run across, they will allow you to make correct diversity calculations.

5. After sampling each of the fields, add the numbers of flowers seen in each area. If the numbers are approximately equal, no further sampling is required. Return to any underrepresented field and walk across it on other paths until all of your fields have roughly equal sample sizes. (Each area should provide at least 100 flowers).

6. Calculate H_1, H_{1max}, and D_1 for each field and compare the results.

6.2   Leaf Shape Diversity

Forests look very different from one another depending on where on earth they are. The Eastern deciduous forest is full of the broad leaves of maple and oak, the temperate rain forest of the Pacific Northwest is all evergreen trees and ferns, and the tropics are filled with an amazing variety of plants. You can calculate leaf shape diversity indices for habitats near you by carrying out the following procedure.

1. Go to a habitat that you select for the initial measurements.

2. Walk into the habitat two paces, close your eyes, and look downwards (or in a direction appropriate to the habitat). Open your eyes; the first plant you focus upon will be the one you use next in the data collection.

3. Find a leaf on that first plant, attach it to a blank sheet of paper and mark a "I"next to it. Take two paces and repeat step 2 above.

4. Examine the new leaf to see if it matches the other one. If it does, add another mark next to the previously attached leaf. If not, attach the new leaf and mark a "I"next to it.

5. Repeat steps 2–5 above until you have scored 100 leaves per habitat.

6. Calculate H_1, H_{1max}, and D_1 for each area selected and compare results. What might account for any differences in these values?

6.3   Student Migrations

Animals migrate with the seasons, as the geese flying south every autumn remind those of us in central New York. Other areas are the scenes of other migrations, like the spectacular flights of monarch butterflies on the west coast as they travel to Mexico. Students also migrate on an annual cycle, from homes in various places to their colleges. You can determine how diverse the set of geographical origins of your institution's student body is by carrying out the following procedure.

1. Go to a student parking lot on your campus. If there are no specifically student-assigned lots, select one that is near the dormitories and as far as possible from any other academic buildings.

2. Walk along a row of cars, scoring the license plates by state or province of origin. Collect scores for 100 or more cars.

3. Carry out a procedure similar to step 2 above, but in the parking lot for a grocery store or mall away from campus. It is usually a good assumption that members of the local population will frequent such a store.

4. Calculate H_1, H_{1max}, and D_1 values for your two data sets and compare the results. What does it tell you about student migrations, and why did you need to collect a second non-student sample in order to interpret your data sets well?

5. Are there any portions of the student population that might be under or over represented by the method used to collect data in step 2? Often, your college catalog, admissions office, or registrar can supply accurate data on the geographical origins of the student population. If you can obtain such data, use it to compute H_1, H_{1max}, and D_1 for the student body and compare the results to your earlier calculations.

7. Solutions to the Exercises

1. $\log_2 9 - \log_2 5 \approx 0.848$.

2. Assume $m > n$, then $m/n > 1$, so $\log_2(m/n) > 0$. Now, if both systems are in states of equiprobability, then

$$H_1(m) - H_1(n) = \log_2 m - \log_2 n = \log_2(m/n) > 0.$$

3. $H_1 \approx 1.237$ bits; $D_1 \approx 0.348$ bits.

4. a) Most diverse: Chinese, $H_1 \approx 1.885$ bits; least diverse: Navajos, $H_1 \approx 0.769$ bits.

  b) Germans: $D_1 \approx 0.284$ bits; Basques: $D_1 \approx 0.941$ bits; Navajos: $D_1 \approx 1.231$ bits; Chinese: $D_1 \approx 0.115$ bits.

5. a) Siamese: $H_1 \approx 1.834$ bits; English: $H_1 \approx 1.419$ bits; Blackfeet Indians: $H_1 \approx 0.786$ bits.

  b) The Blackfeet Indians have the highest divergence, $D_1 \approx 1.214$ bits.

6.

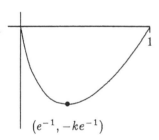

$(e^{-1}, -ke^{-1})$

8. a) Swamps: $H_1 \approx 3.14$ bits; uplands: $H_1 \approx 3.17$ bits.

  b) Swamps: $D_1 \approx 1.32$ bits; uplands: $D_1 \approx 1.29$ bits.

9. a) Bee 1: $H_1 \approx 2.86$ bits; bee 2: $H_1 \approx 2.97$ bits; bee 3: $H_1 \approx 2.60$.

  b) Bee 1: $D_1 \approx 1.14$ bits; bee 2: $H_1 \approx 1.03$ bits; bee 3: $D_1 \approx 1.40$.

10. a) White-crowned sparrows: $H_1 \approx 2.95$ bits; song sparrows: $H_1 \approx 2.21$ bits;

  b) White-crowned sparrows: $D_1 \approx 0.75$ bits; song sparrows: $D_1 \approx 1.49$ bits.

References

Barrett, G. W. 1968. The effects of an acute insecticide stress on a semi-enclosed grassland ecosystem. *Ecology* 49: 1019–1035.

Baylis, J. R. 1976. A quantitative study of long-term courtship: II. A comparative study of the dynamics of courtship in two new world cichlid fishes. *Behaviour* 59: 118–161.

Boyd, W. C. 1939. Blood Groups. *Tabulae Biologicae* 17: 234.

_____. 1950. *Genetics and the Races of Man*. Lexington, MA: D. C. Heath.

Ford, D. 1988. A reporter at large: crown of thorns. *New Yorker* (25 July 1988): 34–63.

Haldane, J .B. S. and H. Spurway. 1954. A statistical analysis of communication in *Apis mellifera* and a comparison with communication in other animals. *Insectes Sociaux* 1: 247–283.

Khinchin, A. I. 1957. *Mathematical Foundations of Information Theory*. New York: Dover.

Kolmes, S. A. 1985. An information-theory analysis of task specialization among worker honey bees performing hive duties. *Animal Behaviour* 33: 181-187.

Lloyd, M., J. H. Zar, and J. R. Karr. 1968. On the calculation of information theoretical measures of diversity. *American Midland Naturalist* 79: 257–272.

MacArthur, R. H., and J. W. MacArthur. 1961. On bird species diversity. *Ecology* 42: 594–598.

Magurran, A. E. 1988. *Ecological Diversity and its Measurement*, Princeton, NJ: Princeton University Press.

Monk, C. D. 1967. Tree species diversity in the eastern deciduous forest with particular reference to north central Florida. *American Naturalist* 101: 173–187.

Odum, E. P. 1971. *Fundamentals of Ecology*, 3rd ed. Philadelphia: W. B. Saunders.

Pielou, E. C. 1975. *Ecological Diversity*. New York: Wiley.

Pielou, E. C. 1984. *The Interpretation of Ecological Data*. New York: Wiley.

Spitler-Nabors, and Baker. 1987. Sexual display response of female white-crowned sparrows to normal, isolate, and modified conspecific songs. *Animal Behaviour* 35: 380–386.

Whitney, G. G. 1986. Relation of Michigan's presettlement pine forests to substrate and disturbance history. *Ecology* 67: 1548–1559.

Wilson, E. O. 1962. Chemicial Communication among workers of the fire ant *Solenopsis saevissima* (Fr. Smith). 2. An information analysis of the odor trail. *Animal Behaviour* 10: 148–158.

About the Authors

Steven Kolmes received his B.S. in zoology from Ohio University and his M.S. and Ph.D. degrees in zoology from the University of Wisconsin at Madison. His main area of interest is the division of labor and ergonomic efficiency in honeybees. He is currently the chair of the Department of Biology at Hobart and William Smith Colleges.

Kevin Mitchell received his B.A. in mathematics and philosophy from Bowdoin College and his Ph.D. in mathematics from Brown University. His main area of interest is algebraic geometry. He is currently the chair of the Department of Mathematics and Computer Science at Hobart and William Smith Colleges.

Hobart and William Smith Colleges' emphasis on and support for multidisciplinary work has permitted both authors to explore new areas, including team-teaching a course entitled "Mathematical Models and Biological Systems," for which this unit was developed.

UMAP

Modules in Undergraduate Mathematics and its Applications

Module 709

A Blood Cell Population Model, Dynamical Diseases, and Chaos

William B. Gearhart
Mario Martelli

Published in cooperation with the Society for Industrial and Applied Mathematics, the Mathematical Association of America, the National Council of Teachers of Mathematics, the American Mathematical Association of Two-Year Colleges, The Institute of Management Sciences, and the American Statistical Association.

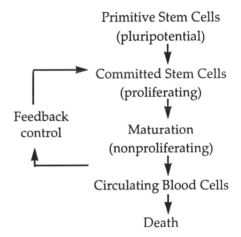

Primitive Stem Cells
(pluripotential)

Committed Stem Cells
(proliferating)

Feedback
control

Maturation
(nonproliferating)

Circulating Blood Cells

Death

Applications of Discrete Dynamical Systems to Medicine

COMAP, Inc. 60 Lowell Street, Arlington, MA (617) 641-2600

INTERMODULAR DESCRIPTION SHEET:	UMAP Unit 709
TITLE:	A Blood Cell Population Model, Dynamical Diseases, and Chaos
AUTHORS:	William B. Gearhart and Mario Martelli Department of Mathematics California State University, Fullerton Fullerton, CA 92634
MATHEMATICAL FIELD:	Discrete Dynamical Systems
APPLICATION FIELD:	Medicine
TARGET AUDIENCE:	Upper-division undergraduates in applied mathematics, biology, and pre-medicine.
ABSTRACT:	This Module gives an introduction to the modeling of blood cell populations and the role of modeling in the study of dynamical diseases of the blood.
PREREQUISITES:	First-year calculus. Some experience with discrete dynamical systems and elementary real analysis would help.
RELATED UNITS:	Unit 553: Graphical Analysis of Some Difference Equations in Mathematical Biology, by M. Eisen.
	Unit 653: The Ricker Salmon Model, by R. Greenwell.
	UMAP Monograph: *Introduction to Population Modeling*, by J.C.Frauenthal.

©Copyright 1990 by COMAP, Inc. All rights reserved.

COMAP, Inc. 60 Lowell St., Arlington, MA 02174 (617) 641–2600

A Blood Cell Population Model Dynamical Diseases, and Chaos

William B. Gearhart
Mario Martelli
Department of Mathematics
California State University, Fullerton
Fullerton, CA 92634

Table of Contents

MODULES AND MONOGRAPHS IN UNDERGRADUATE
MATHEMATICS AND ITS APPLICATIONS (UMAP) PROJECT

The goal of UMAP is to develop, through a community of users and developers, a system of instructional modules in undergraduate mathematics and its applications to be used to supplement existing courses and from which complete courses may eventually be built.

The Project was guided by a National Advisory Board of mathematicians, scientists, and educators. UMAP was funded by a grant from the National Science Foundation and is now supported by the Consortium for Mathematics and Its Applications (COMAP), Inc., a non-profit corporation engaged in research and development in mathematics education.

COMAP Staff

Paul J. Campbell	Editor
Solomon Garfunkel	Executive Director, COMAP
Laurie W. Aragon	Development Director
Philip A. McGaw	Production Manager
Roland Cheyney	Project Manager
Laurie M. Holbrook	Copy Editor
Robin Altomonte	Administrative Asst./Distribution
Dale Horn	Design Assistant

1.   Introduction

Physiological systems of normal mammals display some easily recognized and predictable patterns. In a healthy state, for example, respiration is oscillatory, while blood cell counts are nearly constant.

However, in certain diseases, these patterns change. Systems that normally oscillate may become steady, or may begin to oscillate in a different manner; systems that were steady may begin to oscillate, perhaps in very complicated ways. Such disorders have been called *dynamical diseases* by Glass and Mackey [1979].

Generally, dynamical diseases are particular to physiological control systems, causing them to display abnormal dynamics. A variety of dynamical diseases have been identified in the respiratory system, the blood system, and other areas. In the blood, for example, a type of anemia and certain forms of leukemia have been identified as dynamical diseases. Although laboratory and clinical methods are of primary importance in studying these disorders, it is now recognized that mathematical modeling too is essential to understanding the nature of these diseases and to studying their treatment strategies.

In this Module we will consider the modeling of blood cell populations and show how mathematical modeling is used to explain the behavior and possible origins of dynamical diseases.

The blood cell system and the control mechanisms involved are very complex, and much is not well understood. The development of mathematical models of blood cell populations is quite recent. A number of models have been presented, each depending on the complexities of the blood cell type under study and using advanced mathematical concepts.

The model we consider is simple; its purpose is to illustrate some basic ideas and analysis used in the mathematical modeling of blood cell populations, and to show the interplay between mathematical modeling and the study of dynamical diseases of the blood. Even a first approximation to the dynamical complexity of blood cell populations involves an unexpected wealth of elementary but nontrivial ideas.

In particular, we will present the notion of chaotic behavior, a distinctive feature of many severe diseases. The possibility of the very complex dynamics of chaos was first recognized by Poincaré, but scientists have given it vigorous attention only in recent years. Indeed, chaotic dynamics have been documented in many areas including biology, electronics, and fluid mechanics.

1

2.   A Blood Cell Population Model

We begin with a brief description of the process of blood-cell formation and destruction. We then develop a simple model to describe the dynamics of a blood cell population.

2.1   Blood Cell Formation and Destruction

Blood consists of two basic components: plasma and blood cells. Plasma is the fluid in which the blood cells are suspended. There are three general types of blood cells: red blood cells, white blood cells, and platelets.

Each type of blood cell has special functions. Red cells carry oxygen from the lungs to the body tissues, white cells protect the body from infection, and platelets help in blood clotting. Under normal conditions, the numbers and type of blood cells produced are controlled by the physiological needs at the time. For the red blood cells, oxygen deficiency leads to the production of the hormone erythropoietin, which stimulates development of red blood cells from among the primitive and committed stem cells. Thus, since red blood cells participate in oxygen transport, the red blood cell production rate increases as the number of red blood cells decreases.

With the exception of lymphocytes (a variety of white blood cell produced in lymphatic tissues), blood cells are formed from primitive stem cells resident in the bone marrow. The primitive stem cells are said to be *pluripotential* because they are capable of producing *committed stem cells*, that is, stem cells committed to develop eventually into one of the three cell types (red, white, or platelet). Once formed, the committed stem cells proliferate (through cell division). After a maturation phase, they become mature cells of the given type and enter the blood stream. This formation process takes several days.

For the white-cell line, the processes regulating the number of cells is not completely understood. It is thought that a decrease in the population leads to the production and release of granulopoietin, a hormone which stimulates the proliferative activity of the committed stem cells. However, granulopoietin has not been isolated, and other stimulating factors are known to exist.

Blood cells eventually die, either by natural aging, infection, or disease. For granulocytes, a type of white blood cell, death occurs randomly, with a half-life of about 7 hours. Red blood cells, on the other hand, have a lifetime of about 120 days.

Figure 1 gives a simplified view of the blood cell formation process. The arrows going from the circulating blood compartment to the committed stem cell compartment indicate the (feedback) control of the level of circulating blood cells on the production of new blood cells.

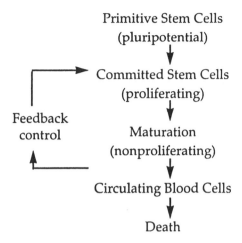

Figure 1. Formation and destruction of blood cells.

2.2   A General Model

We develop now a general model of the dynamics of a blood cell population. Later we will apply this model to red and to white blood cell populations, and also to the pluripotential stem cell population. Our model is necessarily highly simplified, partly so that we can better study its properties, but also because detailed models are very complex, depend substantially on the type of cell, and involve differential-delay equations that require sophisticated qualitative and numerical methods for analysis. Nevertheless, we shall see that this simple model still captures the distinctive features of blood cell population dynamics.

In a normal mammal, the concentration of blood cells is relatively constant or may show small oscillations. However, a blood cell population undergoes continual production and elimination of elements over time. Thus, to model the levels of blood cells, we must consider both production and destruction of cells. Time will be measured in discrete units of length Δ. We will refer to Δ as the *unit time* of the model. Set $t_i = i\Delta$, for $i = 0, 1, 2, \ldots$; and denote by x_i the number of blood cells of a certain type, per kilogram of body weight, at time t_i. Then the general model is given by

$$x_{i+1} - x_i = -d(x_i) + p(x_i),$$

where the function d measures the number of cells destroyed in the time interval t_i to t_{i+1}, and the function p measures the number of cells produced during this time interval. Each function is assumed to depend only on the number of cells at time t_i.

A simple but widely accepted model of destruction for a normal mammal

3

is that during each time interval of length Δ, a constant fraction of cells is destroyed. That is,

$$d(x_i) = cx_i,$$

where c, a unitless constant independent of i and x_i, is called the *destruction coefficient*.

Information about the production function is sketchy. The particular form of the function depends on the type of cell. It is generally agreed that the production rate is a decreasing function over a wide range of cell levels. Indeed, we would expect the production rate to increase when the number of cells decreases. However, there is a critical level of blood cells below which an organism cannot recover without treatment. Also, production becomes unnecessary at high blood-cell levels. Thus, we assume that $p(0) = 0$, that initially the graph of p is increasing, but that after reaching a maximum, the curve decreases to zero. There are many functions that fit this description. For example, in modeling the granulocyte population, Mackey and Glass [1977] have used the function

$$p(x) = \frac{b\theta^m x}{\theta^m + x^m}, \tag{1}$$

where b (unitless), θ (cells/kg), and m (unitless) are positive constants. Lasota [1977] has considered the function

$$p(x) = bx^s e^{-sx/r}, \tag{2}$$

where b, s, and r are positive constants. It is probably the case that the particular algebraic form chosen is not critical, provided a reasonable approximation to the production function is attained.

Supposing that the production function has been determined, the dynamics of the model are given by the iteration scheme

$$x_{i+1} = f(x_i), \qquad \text{for } i = 0, 1, 2, \ldots,$$

where

$$f(x) = (1 - c)x + p(x).$$

We call f the *iteration function* of the model.

This model incorporates a number of simplifications. A precise model would account for cell numbers at the various stages of development, from stem cells to circulating cells in the blood (see, for instance, Rubinow and Lebowitz [1975; 1976]). In addition, the production process involves a significant time delay. Granulocytes, for example, take about six days from the start of production to the appearance of mature cells. Thus the model might be more appropriately written

$$x_{i+1} - x_i = -d(x_i) + p(x_{i-k}),$$

where $k\Delta = \delta$, the delay in production. Including the delay explicitly, although apparently simple, complicates the analysis substantially. In our model, the delay is represented by the unit time Δ. In selecting Δ, then, there are two considerations. We must account for the delay, and also make sure that the assumed form of the destruction function is reasonable, namely, that a constant fraction of cells dies during the time interval Δ.

Under normal (healthy) conditions, the blood cells will attain a level in which the production and destruction of cells occur at equal rates. We will denote this level by v, and refer to it as the *steady-state level*. Thus v is a solution of the equation $d(v) = p(v)$. Equivalently, $v = f(v)$, so that v is a *fixed point* of f.

The destruction coefficient c, the unit time Δ, and the constants in the production function are the parameters of the model. A dynamical disease results when parameter values stray away from those of the healthy state, causing the system to display abnormal dynamics. A mathematical model can help in identifying the nature of the disorder and in studying the effect of treatments. Our task now is to investigate the properties of our model.

Exercises

1. For the production function **(1)**, show that on $(0, \infty)$ there is a single maximum at $x = r_m \theta$ and a single inflection point at $x = s_m \theta$, where

$$r_m = \left(\frac{1}{m-1}\right)^{1/m} \quad \text{and} \quad s_m = \left(\frac{m+1}{m-1}\right)^{1/m}.$$

   Sketch the graph of this production function for $x \geq 0$.

2. For the production function **(2)**, show that on $(0, \infty)$ there is a single maximum at $x = r$. Also show that for $s > 1$ there are inflection points at $x = r(1 \pm \sqrt{1/s})$ while for $0 \leq s \leq 1$ there is a single inflection point at the larger of these two. Sketch the graphs of this production function.

3. For given destruction coefficient c and production function p (either form **(1)** or form **(2)** above), sketch the graphs of $y = cx$ and $y = p(x)$ and locate the steady state v. For definiteness, take $c \in (0, 1]$ and assume the graph of p intersects the line $y = x$ for some $x > 0$. Denote the steady state by v_c. Show that v_c is decreasing as a function of c, and that $v_c \to \infty$ as $c \to 0^+$. Are these properties physically reasonable? Remark: With form **(2)** and $s > 1$, there are two positive solutions of $cx = p(x)$. Later, after introducing the notion of stability, we will see that only the larger solution is physically attainable (see **Exercise 10**).

3.   Parameter Estimation and Model Validation

An important part of model development is verifying that the model reasonably reflects the system it represents. However, validation of models of dynamical diseases is especially difficult. Experimentation with humans, either normal or diseased, is necessarily very limited; and data obtained in clinical settings are approximate and fragmentary, and not designed to aid model verification. While experimentation with animals is a source of information, extending numerical results to humans may be uncertain. Even when data are available, estimating model parameters is doubtful for a system whose output is chaotic and possesses sensitive dependence on initial conditions and parameters. In addition, model parameters may vary substantially from person to person. Thus there are many problems with model verification [Glass and Mackey 1988, Chapter 9].

Still, it is possible to obtain some meaningful numerical data. For example, direct counts of cell concentrations are done routinely. Also, use of tracers to label cells has led to estimates of cell destruction rates and cell production rates (see, for example, Anderson [1983] or Rubinow [1975]). The following examples show how these data can be used to estimate parameters in our model.

Example 1:

For red blood cells, the time from the start of production to the release of mature cells in the blood is about six days. Thus we take the unit time Δ to be 6. Use of tracers indicates that the destruction rate of red blood cells under normal conditions is 2.3% per day [Mackey 1979b]. With $\Delta = 6$ days, we can estimate c as $6 \times 0.023 = 0.14$. In a normal 70-kg man, the red-cell count is about 3.3×10^{11} cells/kg of body weight. This amount is our estimate of the steady-state cell count v. Now, under steady-state conditions, the rate of cell disappearance is $cv = 0.14 \times 3.3 \times 10^{11} = 4.62 \times 10^{10}$ cells/kg; and this amount must equal the steady-state production rate. Hence, we have located a point $(v, 0.14v)$ on the graph of the production function p; that is, $p(v) = 0.14v$.

Next, it is estimated that the maximum production rate is about 10 times the steady state rate, or 4.62×10^{11} cells/kg. This datum locates another point on the graph of p, although the value at which the maximum is attained needs to be determined.

Finally, experiments have found that for rabbits, reduction of the cell population to 75% of the steady-state count results in an increase in production of about 5 times the steady-state rate [Orr et al. 1968]. If we assume this response holds for humans also, then we have a third point on the graph of p, namely, $(0.75v, 5v)$.

6

We will assume that the production function has the form

$$p(x) = v\phi(x/v), \qquad \text{where} \qquad \phi(u) = bu^s e^{-su/r}.$$

Using the three points on the graph of p, we can determine b, r, and s.

The production function has been chosen particularly to simplify the arithmetic. The factor v on the outside of ϕ is used because all the measured production rates are given as multiples of v. The argument of ϕ, that is, x/v, has been chosen so that cell counts are measured in multiples of v, the multiple being the variable u. Thus cells counts can be expressed more simply. Finally, with this form of ϕ, the maximum occurs at $u = r$, allowing us to express the given datum on the maximum production rate more easily.

We obtain the following equations for the parameters.

$$\begin{aligned}
\text{Production at steady state:} && \phi(1) &= be^{-s/r} = 0.14, \\
\text{Maximum production:} && \phi(r) &= br^s e^{-s} = 10 \times 0.14 = 1.4, \\
\text{Production at 75\% of steady state:} && \phi(0.75) &= b(.75)^s e^{-0.75s/r} \\
&& &= 5 \times 0.14 = 0.70.
\end{aligned}$$

With some perseverance, these three equations can be solved for the parameters. For example, one can successively eliminate variables to obtain one equation in one unknown, which can then be solved by an iterative method, such as the bisection method or Newton's method. Approximate solutions are $s = 8$, $r = 0.5$, and $b = 1.1 \times 10^6$.

Example 2:

As mature cells, granulocytes (a type of white blood cell) are found in the blood and are also held in reserve in the marrow. As indicated earlier, the mechanisms regulating the production of these cells are not fully understood. In this example, however, let us assume that the feedback control that stimulates proliferative activity of committed stem cells is based on total cell count in the blood and the marrow reserve. The time from inception of cell production to appearance of mature cells is about six days [Mackey and Glass 1977]. Thus, we take the unit time $\Delta = 6$. The cell destruction rate is about 10% per day [Mackey and Glass 1977; Erslev and Gabuzda 1985]. Hence, $c = 6 \times 0.1 = 0.6$. The steady-state total cell count v is about 8.2×10^9 cells/kg of body weight [Erslev and Gabuzda 1985]. Therefore, the steady-state rate of cell disappearance is

$$cv = 0.6 \times 8.2 \times 10^9 = 4.92 \times 10^9 \text{ cells/kg,}$$

which in turn equals the steady-state production rate. Thus the production function satisfies $p(v) = 0.6v$. Finally, we will estimate the maximum production rate to be twice the production rate in the steady state. This factor is approximately that used by Mackey and Glass [1977].

These data locate two points on the graph of the production function. Assume that the production function has the form

$$p(x) = v\phi(x/v), \qquad \text{where} \qquad \phi(u) = bue^{-u/r}.$$

Then we have

Production at steady state: $\phi(1) = be^{-1/r} = 0.6$,

Maximum production: $\phi(r) = bre^{-1} = 2 \times 0.6 = 1.2$.

Solving these equations for the parameters b and r yields the approximate solutions $r = 0.37$ and $b = 8.7$.

These examples illustrate several of the typical difficulties with parameter estimation in blood-cell population modeling. The available data are few and approximate. Also, some data are obtained from experiments with animals, the results of which may have uncertain application to humans. Of particular concern, however, is that much of the data pertains to the steady state only. But the model is supposed to describe also the behavior of the cell counts when the system is not in the steady state. How can we verify that the model reflects these dynamics?

An important way to study dynamical behavior of the blood cell population in humans is to observe the population when it is diseased. In clinical settings, however, it is not possible to obtain data from controlled experiments, as we could in the laboratory. For example, records of leukemia patients upon entering the City of Hope (a hospital located in the Los Angeles area) show variations in the white blood cell count by a factor of 750. Conditions among patients can vary widely, and hence so do the numerical data obtained.

As pointed out by Glass and Mackey [1988], published data on dynamical behavior are rare. Nevertheless, qualitative features of diseases are well established. Such features include steady states that are higher or lower than normal, or oscillations for which estimates of amplitudes or periods have been made. As one part of model verification, we need to see that the model is capable of displaying these patterns. If not, we certainly have reason to reject the model. It is this aspect of model verification that we will pursue in the next sections. To do so, we must first present some basic results about discrete dynamical systems.

Exercises

4. In **Example 2**, the maximum production rate was taken to be twice the steady-state rate. This factor is known only approximately and could be much higher. With the same production function as in **Example 2**, estimate the parameters using a factor of five instead.

5. The blood system is able to respond within a few hours to a depletion of granulocytes in the blood, with increases coming from the marrow reserve. The number of granulocytes in the marrow reserve is more than ten times that of the blood. As an approximation, we could model the number of granulocytes in the blood, independently of the feedback control to the committed stem cells, at least to study the effect of a small depletion over a short period of time. Let us assume such a model, so that now x_i represents the number of granulocytes in the blood at time t_i. The destruction rate of granulocytes in the blood is about 10% per hour and the steady-state cell count is about 7.0×10^8 cells/kg [Wheldon 1975; Rubinow and Lebowitz 1975]. Assume the maximum production rate is 6 times the steady-state rate [Wheldon 1975]. Taking $\Delta = 3$ hours and using the production function (2) with $s = 1$, estimate the parameters of the model.

4.   Discrete Dynamical Systems

We summarize now some results concerning discrete one-dimensional dynamical systems which will be needed in the sequel [Devaney 1989; Edelstein-Keshet 1988; Eisen 1988; Frauenthal 1979; May 1974; May 1975; Perelson 1980].

4.1   Orbits, Stationary States, and Periodic Orbits

Let I be an interval, and let $f : I \mapsto I$ be a continuously differentiable function. The domain of f may be larger than I, but we are interested only in what happens on I. Points in I will be viewed as representing states of a system. Given $p \in I$, consider the sequence of points $x_0 = p$, $x_1 = f(x_0)$, $x_2 = f(x_1)$, and so on. This sequence x_i represents successive states of the system with initial state p. We shall call this sequence an *orbit* starting from p and denote it by $O(p)$.

The following notation will be convenient. Let f^i denote the composition of f with itself i times; that is, $f^i = f \circ f \circ \cdots \circ f$, i times, where f^0 is defined as the identity: $f^0(x) = x$ for all x. Then we can write $x_i = f^i(p)$, for $i = 0, 1, 2, \ldots$. If $x_1 = p$, i.e., $p = f(p)$, then p is called a *fixed point* of f, or a *stationary state* of the system, since no changes will take place if the initial state is p. If $x_n = p$ for some $n \geq 2$ and $x_i \neq p$ for all $0 < i < n$, then the point p, and the orbit $O(p)$, are called *periodic* with period n. In this case, the system goes repeatedly through the states of $O(p)$ in an orderly manner, and any one of the states could be considered an "initial" state. For each point x_i of the orbit, we have $f^n(x_i) = x_i$. Thus each point in the orbit is a fixed point of f^n.

4.2   Stability of Stationary States and Periodic Orbits

For a system in real life to reside exactly at a stationary state is unlikely, since there will always be minor disturbances that move the system slightly away from the stationary state. The question is: Will the system run away from the stationary state, or will it always tend to come back to the stationary state? We say the stationary state is *unstable* in the first case and *stable* in the second.

Suppose p is a fixed point of f and that $|f'(p)| < 1$. Using the mean value theorem and the continuity of f', we can show there is an interval J, centered at p, such that for any $x \in J$ the sequence of points in the orbit $O(x)$ converges to p (**Exercise 6**). Thus, when $|f'(p)| < 1$, we say p is a *local attractor* of the system, or a *stable fixed point* of f.

On the other hand, suppose that $|f'(p)| > 1$. Then, again using the mean value theorem and the continuity of f', we can show there is an open interval J about p such that for any $x \in J$ there is an integer n, depending on x, such that $f^n(x) \notin J$. It follows that the orbit $O(x)$ contains an infinite number of points outside of J (**Exercise 7**). Thus, when $|f'(p)| > 1$, we say p is a *local repellor* of the system, or an *unstable fixed point* of f.

Consider next a periodic orbit of period n: $p = x_0, x_1, \ldots, x_{n-1}, x_n = p$. As mentioned earlier, each point of the orbit is a fixed point of f^n. By the chain rule, we can show that (**Exercise 8**)

$$(f^n)'(x_i) = (f^n)'(p), \qquad \text{for each } i = 0, 1, 2, \ldots, n - 1.$$

Thus, as regards stability, all points in the orbit behave in the same manner. For instance, suppose first that $|(f^n)'(p)| < 1$. By continuity, there is an open interval J, centered at p, such that for any $x \in J$, $f^{nk}(x) \to p$ as $k \to \infty$. For each i, $0 \le i \le n - 1$, the $(i+1)^{\text{st}}$ point in the orbit $O(x)$ is $f^i(x)$, and every n^{th} point, starting at $f^i(x)$, is given by $f^{nk}(f^i(x))$, for $k = 0, 1, 2, \ldots$. However,

$$f^{nk}(f^i(x)) = f^i(f^{nk}(x)) \to f^i(p) \qquad \text{as } k \to \infty.$$

Thus the orbit $O(x)$ converges to the periodic orbit $O(p)$. We say in this case that the orbit $O(p)$ is a *stable periodic orbit* and will refer to the set $O(p)$ as a *local attractor*. In the event that p is an unstable fixed point of f^n, we can argue in a similar way, but with somewhat more elaborate reasoning, that $O(p)$ is an *unstable periodic orbit*, and refer to the set $O(p)$ as a *local repellor*.

4.3   Chaotic Orbits

We shall say an orbit $O(x)$ is *asymptotically periodic* if there is a periodic orbit $O(p)$ such that

$$|f^i(x) - f^i(p)| \to 0 \qquad \text{as } i \to \infty.$$

In other words, an orbit is asymptotically periodic if it converges to a periodic orbit. In the previous subsection we encountered an asymptotically periodic orbit. If we start at a point that is sufficiently near a stable periodic orbit, then its orbit converges to the periodic orbit. An asymptotically periodic orbit behaves with some predictability, but an orbit that is not asymptotically periodic appears random. We shall refer to a bounded orbit that is not asymptotically periodic as *chaotic*.

Further motivation for this definition is found by considering the limit points of an orbit. A point q is a *limit point for a sequence* x_i if there is a subsequence that converges to q. For $p \in I$, let $L(p)$ denote the set of limit points of the orbit $O(p)$. Then we have the following result:

Theorem 1. *A bounded orbit that is not asymptotically periodic has infinitely many limit points.*

A brief proof: The sets $O(p)$ and $f(O(p))$ differ only by the point p. Thus, they have the same limit points; and hence, when $O(p)$ is bounded, $L(p) = f(L(p))$; that is to say, $L(p)$ is invariant under f.

Now, suppose $L(p)$ is finite. Then there is no proper subset of $L(p)$ that is invariant under f, and therefore $L(p)$ must be a periodic orbit (**Exercise 9**). Since $O(p)$ converges to $L(p)$, the orbit $O(p)$ is asymptotically periodic. Thus, any bounded orbit with finitely many limit points is asymptotically periodic, and the theorem follows. $\square$

The definition of a chaotic orbit has intuitive appeal, but it does not tell us how to recognize a chaotic orbit. However, T.Y. Li and J.A. Yorke proved a remarkable result, which in conjunction with a result obtained by A.N. Sharkovsky, can be rephrased as follows:

Theorem 2 [Li and Yorke 1975; Sharkovsky 1964]. *Let $f : I \mapsto I$ be continuous and have an orbit of period $2n + 1$ for some positive integer n. Then f has a fixed point and orbits of every period $m \geq 2n + 1$ and of every even period $k \leq 2n$. Moreover, there is an uncountable subset S of I such that for each $p \in S$, the orbit $O(p)$ is chaotic.*

We will use this result for $n = 1$. The theorem then states that the existence of an orbit of period 3 implies there are orbits of all periods and that there are uncountably many chaotic orbits. Li and Yorke [1975] show further that an orbit of period 3 exists when there are points $a \in I$, $b = f(a)$, $c = f(b)$, and $d = f(c)$ such that $d \leq a < b < c$ or $d \geq a > b > c$. An elegant and simple way to obtain the above results, except for existence of chaotic orbits, has been discovered by P.D. Straffin, Jr. [1978].

Exercises

6. Let I be an interval and $f : I \mapsto R$ be continuous together with its first derivative. Suppose $p \in I$ is a fixed point of f and $|f'(p)| < 1$. Show there is an interval J centered at p such that $f^i(x) \to p$ as $i \to \infty$, for any $x \in J$.

7. Assume the same conditions as the previous problem, except that $|f'(p)| > 1$. Show there is an interval J centered at p such that for each $x \in J$, there is an n, depending on x, for which $f^n(x)$ lies outside J. Hence conclude that for $x \in J$, the orbit $O(x)$ has an infinite number of points outside J.

8. Let I be an interval and $f : I \mapsto R$ be differentiable. Assume $O(p)$ is periodic with period n. Prove that for each $i = 0, 1, 2, \ldots, n-1$, $(f^n)'(x_i) = (f^n)'(p)$, where $x_i = f^i(p)$ is the $(i+1)^{\text{st}}$ point in the orbit.

9. For an orbit $O(p)$, suppose $L(p)$ is finite and has no proper subset that is invariant under f. Show that $L(p)$ is a periodic orbit.

10. Consider the iteration function $f(x) = (1 - c)x + p(x)$, where the production function is **(2)** with $s > 1$ (as in **Example 1** for the red blood cell population). For definiteness, take $c \in (0, 1]$ and assume the line $y = x$ intersects the graph of p.

   a) Sketch the graph of f and show there are two positive fixed points. Denote the smaller by u_c and the larger by v_c.

   b) Show that u_c is unstable for all c. Show also that any orbit which starts below u_c will converge to 0, while an orbit that starts just above u_c will initially move upward toward v_c. Remark: Thus we interpret u_c as the minimal number of blood cells needed by the organism to survive.

   c) Show that v_c may be either stable or unstable, but that it is stable when c is sufficiently small. Remark: We interpret v_c as the steady state. If the destruction coefficient c is too large, the steady state may become unstable, as we shall see in the next section.

11. Write the production function **(2)** as in **Example 1** and show that the derivative of the iteration function at the steady state v is

$$f'(v) = 1 - c + cs\left(1 - \frac{1}{r}\right).$$

Thus show that in **Examples 1** and **2** the steady states are stable.

5.   Qualitative Analysis and Applications of the Model

We are prepared now to study the dynamical behavior of our model, and in particular how well it reflects properties of certain dynamical diseases. Such studies assist not only with model validation but also in testing hypotheses concerning origins of the disease.

5.1   Hemolytic Anemia

The red blood cells contain the protein hemoglobin, which combines with oxygen in the lungs and carries it through the blood to the tissues. Anemia is a condition in which the amount of hemoglobin or the number of red blood cells is below normal levels. Anemia may result from insufficient production of hemoglobin, as in iron-deficiency anemia, or by defective hemoglobin, as in sickle-cell anemia. It can also occur from the premature destruction of red blood cells, a disorder called *hemolytic anemia*. This premature destruction may happen because the red blood cells are defective or the body produces antibodies that attack the red blood cells, or it may be caused under certain conditions by drugs or infection.

Experiments have shown that the induction of hemolytic anemia in rabbits can result sometimes in steady depressed levels of hemoglobin, and at other times in *sustained oscillations* in hemoglobin concentrations and numbers of reticulocytes (a type of red blood cell) [Orr et al. 1968]. Can our model account for this behavior? In particular, is it possible that simply an increased destruction coefficient explains these observations?

Write the iteration function as

$$f_c(x) = (1 - c)x + p(x),$$

with the subscript c to indicate dependence on the destruction coefficient. We will consider values of c in the interval $(0, 1]$. In **Example 1**, a production function of the form **(2)** with $s > 1$ was determined for the red blood cells. However, in the analysis to follow, only certain properties of this function will be needed. We will assume the graph of p has the same shape as the production function in **Example 1**; in particular, we will require three assumptions **(A)**, **(B)**, and **(C)**.

(A). *p is differentiable, $p'(0) = 0$, and p has exactly two inflection points, which lie above the line $y = x$.*

Under this first assumption, f_c has two positive fixed points. Denote the smaller by u_c and the larger by v_c. Then, recalling **Exercise 10**, we know that u_c is unstable for any $c > 0$, but v_c is stable for sufficiently small c and represents the steady state. In **Example 1**, we saw that c near 0.1 to 0.2 is normal. Over this range, v_c is stable (**Exercise 11**). For $c \in (0, 1]$, $v_1 \leq v_c < \infty$, and v_c is monotonically decreasing as a function of c, with $v_c \to \infty$ as $c \to 0^+$, and $v_c \to v_1$ as $c \to 1^-$ (**Exercise 3**).

We will further require that

(B). $p'(v_1) < -1$.

The production function for red blood cells calculated in **Example 1** satisfies these assumptions (**Exercises 12 and 13**).

Theorem 3. *Let* $f_c(x) = (1-c)x + p(x)$, *and suppose that the production function* p *satisfies* **(A)** *and* **(B)**, *so that* f_c *has positive fixed points* u_c *(the smaller) and* v_c *(the larger). Then there exists a unique value of* c *in* $(0, 1)$, *say* c_α, *which satisfies* $f_c'(v_c) = -1$. *For* $c \in (0, c_\alpha)$, *the point* v_c *is stable; and for* $c \in (c_\alpha, 1]$, v_c *is unstable.*

Proof: Observe first that $f_c'(v_c) = -1$ if and only if $p'(v_c) = -2 + c$. Consider now the graph of p' in **Figure 2**. For small $c > 0$, the point labeled A lies to the left of the point labeled B. As c increases toward 1, A moves to the right and B moves to the left. There will be exactly one value $c = c_\alpha$ at which A and B coincide, and at this value of c we have $f_c'(v_c) = -1$.

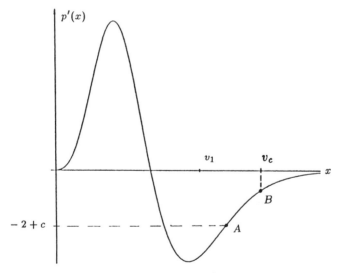

Figure 2. Graph of p'.

Suppose now that $c \in (0, c_\alpha)$. Then $v_c > v_{c_\alpha}$, and $-2 + c < -2 + c_\alpha$. Thus,

$$-2 + c < -2 + c_\alpha = p'(v_{c_\alpha}) < p'(v_c),$$

so that $-1 < (1 - c) + p'(v_c) = f_c'(v_c)$. But since $p'(v_c) < 0$, we have also $f_c'(v_c) < 1 - c < 1$. Thus $|f_c'(v_c)| < 1$, so that v_c is stable. An analogous argument shows that v_c is unstable when $c > c_\alpha$. $\square$

Thus, provided the destruction coefficient is not too large (less than c_α), the model shows that the steady state is stable. However, whenever c is greater than this threshold value c_α, the steady state is unstable.

Theorem 4. *Let f and p be as in Theorem 3, and let c_α be the unique value of c such that $f_c'(v_c) = -1$. Then, for any $c > c_\alpha$, there exist points of period two.*

Proof: Let $c > c_\alpha$. The graph of f_c^2 intersects the line $y = x$ at u_c and at v_c. But if x is either u_c or v_c, then

$$\frac{d}{dx} f_c^2(x) > 1.$$

Thus, just to the right of u_c, the graph of f_c^2 lies above the line $y = x$; but just to the left of v_c, it lies below the line $y = x$. Therefore, by continuity, there exists a point between u_c and v_c which has period two. $\square$

We now see that when the destruction coefficient is too large (bigger than c_α), periodic solutions arise. In fact, with the production function for the red blood cells determined in **Example 1**, we find numerically that as c increases, "period doubling" occurs; that is, as c increases, orbits of periods $2, 4, 8, \ldots$ arise, until an orbit of period 3 appears. The occurrence of periodic solutions may explain the observed oscillations in the experiments of Orr et al. [1968]. However, further analysis of the model indicates that cell counts could have followed a chaotic orbit. To see this, we make one more technical assumption concerning the production function. For $c \in (0, 1]$, let y_c denote the point at which f_c attains its local maximum. Then we assume

(C). $p^2(y_1) < u_1$, *where for $c \in (0, 1]$, u_c is the smaller positive fixed point of f.*

This assumption might be expected. When $c = 1$, the system will try to compensate for the high destruction rate with greatly increased production. Initially, a very large number of cells enters the blood stream. The system senses this excessive accumulation; and during the next time interval, only a small number of cells is released. Consequently the cell count falls below the critical level u_1.

Theorem 5. *Let f and p be as in Theorem 3. Suppose the production function satisfies also assumption **(C)**. Then there exists $c_\beta \in (0, 1)$ such that for any $c \in (c_\beta, 1]$, f_c has a point of period three, and hence there are uncountably many chaotic orbits.*

Proof: For $c \in (0, 1]$, there is a point a_c between u_c and y_c such that $f_c(a_c) = y_c$ (a sketch of the graph of f_c shows this result). Assumption **(C)** implies there is $c_\beta \in (0, 1)$ such that for any $c \in (c_\beta, 1]$, we have $f_c^2(y_c) < u_c$, since $u_c \to u_1$, and $y_c \to y_1$, as $c \to 1^-$. For $c \in (c_\beta, 1]$, define $d_c = f_c(y_c)$ and $e_c = f_c(d_c)$. Then we have $e_c < a_c < y_c < d_c$, and therefore the conditions of the Li and Yorke theorem are satisfied. $\square$

15

Under the conditions of **Theorem 5**, the iteration function f_c, for sufficiently large c, has an uncountable number of chaotic orbits. A direct calculation shows that the production function for red blood cells of **Example 1** satisfies **(C)**. The model thus indicates that for large destruction rates, the cell counts are likely to follow chaotic orbits.

Exercises

12. Show that the production function determined in **Example 1** satisfies assumption **(A)**. Suggestion: Show that x is an inflection point of p if and only if x/v is an inflection point of ϕ, and hence that p satisfies assumption **(A)** if ϕ does. Check assumption **(A)** for ϕ directly, using the results of **Exercise 2**.

13. Show that the production function of **Example 1** satisfies assumption **(B)**. Suggestion: Set $w_1 = v_1/v$, and using the fact that $w_1 = \phi(w_1)$, show that $p'(v_1) = 8(1 - 2w_1)$. Then show that $w_1 > 9/16$.

14. The proof of **Theorem 4** rests on the fact that when $c > c_\alpha$, the derivative of f_c^2 is greater than 1 at at u_c and at v_c. Verify this result.

5.2   Chronic Myelogenous Leukemia

Chronic myelogenous leukemia (CML) is a cancer of the white blood cells, characterized by an excessive increase in granulocytes in the marrow and blood. The cells produced are abnormal, and counts in the marrow may be 150 times the normal. Further, the overaccumulation disrupts production of the other blood cells and interferes with various organs. There is evidence that the disorder resides in the primitive stem cells [Erslev and Gabuzda 1985]. In recent years, some clinical reports have indicated a periodic variant in which cell counts oscillate around elevated levels, with a period of 30–70 days depending on the patient [Glass and Mackey 1979].

To investigate whether the model can explain these observations, we apply it to the primitive stem cell population. This population is self-maintaining. When primitive stem cells differentiate to form committed stem cells, the number of primitive stem cells decreases. This decrease causes new cells to be produced through mitosis (cell division) of remaining cells. Cells that are not in the proliferative phase are said to be resting. Committed stem cells can come only from resting cells.

The mechanisms and feedback control processes in CML are not fully understood. However, it is believed that in CML the primitive stem cell compartment consists of two populations, the normal cells and the leukemic cells. Each is thought to be governed by the same dynamics, but with different parameters.

We will apply the model to the leukemic population. Now x_i denotes the number of resting primitive stem cells (leukemic) at time t_i. Recall that our model specifies $f(x) = (1-c)x + p(x)$. The destruction coefficient c is now the fraction of primitive stem cells that leave to become committed cells during a time interval of length Δ. For the production function, we follow Mackey [1979a] and use **(1)**:

$$p(x) = \frac{b\theta^m x}{\theta^m + x^m},$$

with positive parameters b, θ, and m. Thus we are assuming that during the time interval from t_i to t_{i+1}, the number of cells that leave the proliferative phase to enter the resting state is $p(x_i)$. For the normal human, it has been estimated that

$$
\begin{aligned}
c &= \gamma\Delta, & \text{with } \gamma = 0.16 \text{ per day,}\\
b &= \beta\Delta, & \text{with } \beta = 1.43 \text{ per day,}\\
\theta &= 3.22 \times 10^8 \text{ cells/kg,}\\
m &= 3,
\end{aligned}
$$

with a delay time in production of Δ = 0.68 days [Mackey 1979a].

Our goal is to study possible explanations for the observed increases and oscillations in the cell count. We need first to express the steady-state cell count as a function of the parameters. Letting v denote the steady state level, we have $cv = p(v)$. Solving for v yields

$$v = \theta \left(\frac{\beta}{\gamma} - 1 \right)^{1/m}.$$

At first thought, the logical explanation for increased cell counts would be an increase in the magnitudes of the production function, which means an increase in the parameter β. However, assuming that all other variables remain unchanged, we see from the expression for v that to achieve a 50-fold increase in v would require, in view of the cube root (m = 3), an increase in β by a factor of approximately 50^3 = 125,000. Although leukemic cells are known to proliferate much faster than normal cells, such an enormous increase in β seems unlikely.

Examination of the expression for v, however, suggests that a simpler possibility is an increase in θ. A 50-fold increase in v would require only a 50-fold increase in θ. In the expression for the production function, increasing θ leads to an elongation of the graph of p and an increase in the maximum. This means there are higher production levels that extend over a wider range of the population cell counts. Thus, CML may involve an alteration in the feedback control process of primitive stem cell replacement.

Increase in the parameter θ seems the likely reason for increased cell levels. However, does this increase also explain the 30- to 70-day oscillations in cell counts observed in some patients? This question requires that we examine the stability of the steady state v. To begin, we need an expression for $f'(v)$, the slope of the iteration function at the steady state. Using the result of **Exercise 1** for the derivative of f and substituting the expression for v yields

$$f'(v) = 1 - cm + \frac{c^2 m}{b}.$$

But this expression does not depend on the parameter θ. Moreover, for the given parameter values, $f'(v) = 0.71$, showing that the steady state is stable for any value of θ. Thus an increase in θ does not help us understand the oscillations that have been observed.

However, there is another possibility. In CML, evidence indicates that for myeloblasts, a committed (white) stem cell, the time spent in the proliferative phase is longer than for normal cells. This evidence suggests that the unit time Δ in the model may be greater than usual. Consider, then, an arbitrary delay time Δ. With $c = \gamma \Delta$ and $b = \beta \Delta$, we can express f' in terms of Δ as

$$f'(v) = 1 - \gamma m \Delta + \frac{\gamma^2 m \Delta}{\beta}.$$

Substituting the estimated values of γ, β, and m, we get $f'(v) = 1 - 0.43\Delta$. Thus, for Δ greater that $2/0.43 = 4.7$ days, the steady state would be unstable. As Δ increases beyond this value, an orbit of period two arises. In this case, a period of two is $2 \times 4.7 \approx 9$ days, which agrees with the 12 days calculated by Mackey using a more detailed model [Mackey 1979a]. It appears that the increased delay time of the leukemic cells is the likely source of oscillations in cell counts.

We see now that the model *is* able to reflect the dynamics of CML, giving further support for the assumptions that comprise the model. In addition, the analysis offers insights into the possible malfunctions that occur in the disorder.

Exercises

15. Verify the stated effect of increasing θ on the shape of the production function. The results of **Exercise 1** help.

16. Show that when Δ exceeds 4.7 days, orbits of period two arise. Suggestion: Use the same proof as in **Theorem 4**, with the two fixed points of the iteration function here being 0 and v.

6.   Conclusion

We have given an introduction to the mathematical modeling of blood cell populations. The model is simple, and more-precise and detailed models are under study. Certainly, a better understanding of the mechanisms, especially in quantitative terms, of blood-cell formation and destruction is needed. The problems of parameter estimation and model verification are formidable.

To some extent, of course, confidence in a model comes with a knowledge of the cellular and biochemical processes involved. However, hard data are also needed; and for our situation, little data have been obtained to serve model verification. But it is not premature to proceed with model development. Good models are available now; new laboratory and clinical results can help refine them. At the same time, analysis of the models tells us what dynamical phenomena to look for and how to design experiments and studies. Moreover, models can be used to test hypotheses regarding possible mechanisms, and are thus tools for investigation. Ultimately, models will help us study treatment strategies for diseases.

A major step forward would be the development of closer ties between those on the laboratory and clinical sides of research and those interested in mathematical modeling. Glass and Mackey [1979] noted:

> The existence of classifiable dynamical diseases in humans suggests a corresponding rich theory of bifurcations in nonlinear ordinary, partial, and functional differential equations which model physiological control systems. At this point, a sufficient body of data is not yet available for actual testing of theories of dynamical diseases. In our view, close collaboration between theorists and clinicians is needed to clarify the bases of these dynamical diseases.

We can only echo this plea, and hope that this Module will help stimulate interest in the modeling of blood cell populations.

7.   Sample Exam

1. Let $f : I \mapsto I$ be continuous. Suppose that for some $p \in I$, the orbit $O(p)$ converges. Show that the limit is a fixed point of f.

2. Let $f : [a, b] \mapsto R$ be continuous. Assume that $[a, b]$ is contained in the image of f. Prove that f has a fixed point in $[a, b]$. Suggestion: Consider the function $g(x) = x - f(x)$.

19

3. Let I be an interval and let $f : I \mapsto I$ be continuous. Assume there is a point $a \in I$ such that: $a < f(a) < f^3(a)$, $f^4(a) = a$, and f is increasing on $[a, f(a)]$. Prove that there is an orbit of period three. Suggestion: Consider the image of the interval $[a, f(a)]$ under f^3 and use the result of the previous problem.

4. Consider the model of **Exercise 5** for the granulocytes in the blood. The destruction rate is 10% per hour, and the steady-state cell count is 7.0 $\times$ 10^8 cells/kg. Let the unit time be $\Delta = 3$ hours, and the maximum production be 10 times the steady-state rate.

   a) Use the production function **(2)** with $s = 1$ and estimate the parameters of the model.

   b) Is the steady state stable?

   c) As mentioned in **Exercise 5**, the blood system can respond to a depletion of granulocytes in the blood within a few hours, with cells coming from the marrow reserve. In fact, within two or three hours, the number of blood granulocytes becomes somewhat larger than normal, and then returns shortly to the normal steady state (with perhaps some oscillation in the process). Is the above model consistent with this behavior? Suggestion: Consider the graph of the iteration function. Show how points in an orbit will behave when the initial point lies just below the steady state.

5. Consider the model of **Example 2** for the regulation of granulocytes. For a unit time Δ (days), the destruction coefficient is $c = \gamma\Delta$, with $\gamma = 0.1$, and the production function has the form

$$p(x) = bxe^{-x/q}, \qquad \text{where } b = \beta\Delta.$$

The calculations in **Example 2** indicated that $\beta \approx 1.5$ for a normal system.

   a) Show that the steady-state cell count is $v = q\ln\left(\frac{\beta}{\gamma}\right)$.

   b) Show that the slope of the iteration function f at the steady-state is

$$f'(v) = 1 - \gamma\Delta\ln\left(\frac{\beta}{\gamma}\right).$$

   c) Suppose hypothetically that in chronic or acute myelogenous leukemia, the regulation of leukemic cells in the marrow reserve and blood were to follow the same model as in **Example 2** but with different parameters than those of the normal cells. Perform an analysis with this model, as was done in Section 5.2 for the primitive stem cells, in order to explain the excessive cell numbers and the oscillations in cell counts.

8.   Solutions to the Exercises

1. The first and second derivatives of the function **(1)** are

$$p'(x) = \frac{b\theta^m[\theta^m - (m-1)x^m]}{(\theta^m + x^m)^2},$$

$$p''(x) = \frac{bm\theta^m x^{m-1}[(m-1)x^m - (m+1)\theta^m]}{(\theta^m + x^m)^3},$$

from which the results follow.

2. The first and second derivatives of the function **(2)** are

$$p'(x) = bsx^{s-1}\left(1 - \frac{x}{r}\right)e^{-sx/r},$$

$$p''(x) = bsx^{s-2}\left(-1 + s\left(1 - \frac{x}{r}\right)^2\right)e^{-sx/r},$$

from which the results follow.

3. The slope of the line $y = cx$ decreases as c decreases. Thus, since p is positive and asymptotic to zero, v_c must increase as c decreases, and $v_c \to \infty$ as $c \to 0^+$. These results are reasonable physically: As the destruction rate decreases, with a fixed production function, the steady-state number of cells would be expected to increase. Of course, the body has only a finite capacity and could not survive a small cell destruction rate.

4. Following **Example 2**, the equations for the parameters are now $be^{-1/r} = 0.6$ and $bre^{-1} = 5 \times 0.6 = 3.0$. Approximate solutions are $r = 0.25$, $b = 33$.

5. With $\Delta = 3$ hours, $c = 3 \times 0.1 = 0.3$, and the production function $p(x) = v\phi(x/v)$, where $\phi(u) = bue^{-u/r}$, the two equations for the parameters r and b are $be^{-1/r} = 0.3$ and $bre^{-1} = 1.8$. Approximate solutions are $r = 0.24$, $b = 21$.

6. Select $d > 0$ so that $|f'(x)| \le m < 1$ for all $x \in J = [p - d, p + d]$. Fix $x_0 \in J$ and consider the orbit $O(x_0)$. For $i = 0, 1, 2, \ldots$, let $x_i = f^i(x_0)$ be the $(i+1)^{st}$ point in the orbit. Suppose that $x_i \in J$ for some $i \ge 0$. By the mean value theorem, we have

$$x_{i+1} - p = f(x_i) - f(p) = f'(t)(x_i - p), \qquad \text{for some } t \in J.$$

Therefore, $|x_{i+1} - p| \le m|x_i - p|$, so that $x_{i+1} \in J$. Thus, by induction, the orbit lies in J, and moreover we have

$$|x_i - p| \le m^i|x_0 - p|, \qquad \text{for each } i \ge 0.$$

Thus, the orbit converges to p.

7. Proceed exactly as in **Exercise 6** as far as the first displayed equation. Then, using the hypothesis, we have

$$|x_{i+1} - p| \geq m^{k+1}|x_0 - p|.$$

Thus, there must be a point in the orbit that lies outside J. Further, if some future point in the orbit should return to J, then by the above argument, in a finite number of steps the orbit will again leave J. Thus, an infinite number of points of the orbit are outside J.

8. By repeated application of the chain rule (or induction, to be rigorous), we get

$$(f^n)'(x_i) = f'(x_i)f'(x_{i+1})\ldots f'(x_{i+n-1}),$$

and

$$(f^n)'(p) = f'(p)f'(x_1)\ldots f'(x_{n-1}).$$

Since the orbit is periodic with period n, it follows that these two expressions are the same.

9. Suppose $L(p)$ has n points. Select any $x_0 \in L(p)$ and form the points x_i by $x_{i+1} = f(x_i)$ for $i = 0, 1, 2, \ldots, n-1$. Each of these points is in $L(p)$ since $L(p)$ is invariant under f. But the points $x_0, x_1, \ldots, x_{n-1}$ must be distinct, otherwise there would be a proper subset of $L(p)$ which is invariant under f. Hence $x_n = p$, so that $L(p)$ is a periodic orbit.

10. **a)** The graph of f lies above the line $y = (1-c)x$, is tangent to this line at $x = 0$ since $p'(0) = 0$, and approaches this line asymptotically as $x \to \infty$ since p is asymptotic to zero. Thus the graph of f lies below the line $y = x$ in a neighborhood of the origin, and also for sufficiently large x. However, the graph of f lies above the line $y = x$ for some x. Hence f must have two positive fixed points.

   b) The slope of f at u_c must be greater than 1 since the graph of f is passing across the line $y = x$ from below. Hence the smaller fixed point is unstable. Any orbit that starts below u_c must form a decreasing sequence, since $f(x) < x$ for all $x \in (0, u_c)$. Hence the orbit converges to a point $q \in [0, u_c)$. By continuity of f, $q = f(q)$. But the only point in $[0, u_c)$ which satisfies this equation is $q = 0$. Finally, any orbit that starts just to the right of u_c will initially move away from u_c toward v_c, since $f(x) > x$ when x lies just to the right of u_c.

   c) The point v_c may or may not be stable, depending on steepness of the production function. However, for a given production function, it will be stable when c is sufficiently small, since the graph of p approaches the x-axis asymptotically.

11. As in **Example 1**, set $p(x) = v\phi(x/v)$. Then

$$f'(x) = 1 - c + p'(x) = 1 - c + \phi'(x/v).$$

But

$$\phi(u) = bu^s e^{-su/r}, \quad \text{so that} \quad \phi'(u) = bsu^{s-1}\left(1 - \frac{u}{r}\right)e^{-su/r}.$$

Now

$$f'(v) = 1 - c + \phi'(1) = 1 - c + bs\left(1 - \frac{1}{r}\right)e^{-s/r}.$$

However, at the steady state, $cv = p(v)$, or $c = \phi(1) = be^{-s/r}$. Thus

$$f'(v) = 1 - c + cs\left(1 - \frac{1}{r}\right).$$

Finally, substituting the parameter values, as calculated in the examples, we find that for **Example 1**, $f'(v) = -0.26$, and for **Example 2**, $f'(v) = -0.62$.

12. Since $p''(x) = \phi''(x/v)/v$, the statement in the suggestion is valid. Thus, it suffices to check that $\phi(u) > u$ at each inflection point of ϕ. Using the result of **Exercise 2**, the inflection points of ϕ are 0.323 and 0.677. Substituting, we get $\phi(0.677) = 0.96$ and $\phi(0.323) = 0.74$. Hence, assumption **(A)** is satisfied.

13. We have $p'(x) = \phi'(x/v)$, and from the solution of **Exercise 2**,

$$\phi'(u) = bsu^{s-1}\left(1 - \frac{u}{r}\right)e^{-su/r}.$$

Hence

$$p'(v) = \phi'(w_1) = bsw_1^{s-1}\left(1 - \frac{w_1}{r}\right)e^{-sw_1/r}.$$

But $w_1 = \phi(w_1)$ gives

$$w_1 = bw_1^s e^{-sw_1/r}, \quad \text{or} \quad 1 = bw_1^{s-1}e^{-sw_1/r}.$$

Hence

$$p'(v) = s\left(1 - \frac{w_1}{r}\right).$$

Since $s = 8$ and $r = 0.5$, we get $p'(v) = 8(1 - 2w_1)$. Finally, to show that $w_1 > 9/16$, it suffices to check by direct calculation that $\phi(9/16) > 9/16$.

14. By the chain rule,

$$(f_c^2)'(x) = f_c'(f_c(x))f_c'(x).$$

Let x be either u_c or v_c. Then $x = f_c(x)$, so that

$$(f_c^2)'(x) = f_c'(x)f_c'(x) = (f_c'(x))^2.$$

Further, when $c > c_\alpha$, $|f_c'(x)| > 1$. Hence the conclusion follows.

15. Using the results of **Exercise 1**, we see that the maximum point, the inflection point, and the distance between them are proportional to θ. Thus, the graph becomes elongated as θ increases. Also, the value of the function at the maximum point is proportional to θ, so the maximum value increases as well.

16. When Δ exceeds 4.7, then the derivative of the iteration function f at the steady state is greater than 1 (by construction). But f also has a fixed point at $x = 0$. The derivative of f is

$$f'(x) = (1 - \gamma\Delta) + \frac{\beta\Delta\theta^m[\theta^m - (m-1)x^m]}{(\theta^m + x^m)^2},$$

so that $f'(0) = 1 + (\beta - \gamma)\Delta > 1$. The proof of **Theorem 4** now applies directly.

9. Solutions to the Sample Exam

1. Let $x_i = f^i(p)$ be the $(i+1)^{st}$ point of the orbit and suppose $x_i \to q$ as $i \to \infty$. Then $x_{i+1} = f(x_i)$ for each $i \geq 0$. Taking limits of both sides as $i \to \infty$ in this last equation, and using the continuity of f, gives $q = f(q)$.

2. Set $g(x) = x - f(x)$. Since $[a, b]$ is contained in its image under f, it follows there are x_1 and x_2 in $[a, b]$ such that $g(x_1) \leq 0$ and $g(x_2) \geq 0$. By the intermediate value theorem, g has a root in $[a, b]$, which is the same as saying that f has a fixed point in $[a, b]$.

3. The interval $[a, f(a)]$ is contained in its image under f^3. Therefore, by the previous problem, there is a point $y \in (a, f(a)]$ that is a fixed point of f^3. Since f is increasing on $[a, f(a)]$, for each point $x \in (a, f(a)]$, $f(x) > f(a) \geq x$, and therefore y could not be a fixed point of f. Further, y could not be a point of period two; that is, $f^2(y) = y$, for then we would have $f^3(y) = f(y) \neq y$. Thus y is a point of period 3.

4. **a)** Following **Example 2**, the production function is written

$$p(x) = v\phi(x/v), \qquad \text{where} \qquad \phi(u) = bue^{-x/r}.$$

The two equations for the parameters are $\phi(1) = be^{-1/r} = 0.3$ and $\phi(r) = bre^{-1} = 10 \times 0.3 = 3$. The solutions are $r = 0.20$, $b = 45$.

b) The derivative of the iteration function at the steady state v is $f'(v) = 1 - c/r = 1 - 0.3/0.2 = -0.5$, so that the steady state is stable.

c) The model is consistent with this behavior. The steady state is stable, and the slope of the iteration function at the steady state is negative. If an orbit starts at a point just below the steady state, then the second point in the orbit will be larger than the steady state, and the remaining iterates will then oscillate around the steady state as they converge to it. Remark: If the slope at the steady state had turned out to be positive, the observation about granulocyte numbers exceeding the steady state after depletion would have given us grounds to reject the model.

5. **a)** At the steady state, $cv = p(v) = bve^{-v/q}$. Dividing by v and taking the natural logarithm of both sides yield the given expression.

b) The iteration function is $f(x) = (1 - c)x + bxe^{-x/q}$, so that

$$f'(x) = 1 - c + b\left(1 - \frac{x}{q}\right)e^{-x/q}.$$

From part (a), $c = be^{-v/q}$, which gives

$$f'(v) = 1 - c + c\left(1 - \frac{v}{q}\right) = 1 - c\ln\left(\frac{\beta}{\gamma}\right),$$

as required.

c) Although an increase in the production parameter β is the logical choice for explaining the increased cell numbers, the slow increase of the natural logarithm function indicates that cell numbers are insensitive to increases in β. However, from the expression for v, the simplest explanation for increased cell levels is an increase in the parameter q. Nevertheless, the expression in part (b) shows that q does not effect the stability of the steady state. However, an increase in Δ could explain the oscillations in the number of leukemic cells. For the given values $\beta = 1.5$ and $\gamma = 0.1$, we get $f'(v) = 1 - 0.27\Delta$. Setting this expression equal to -1 shows that the steady state becomes unstable when Δ passes through $2/0.27 = 7.4$ (days). At this point, periodic orbits of period two arise, and the length of the period would be $2 \times 7.4 = 15$ days. Interestingly, this period, which was obtained from data for the circulating and marrow reserve granulocytes, is about the same as obtained from using independent data for the primitive stem cells.

References

Anderson, D.H. 1983. *Compartmental Modeling and Tracer Kinetics*. Berlin: Springer-Verlag.

Devaney, Robert L. 1989. *An Introduction to Chaotic Dynamical Systems*. 2nd ed. Reading, MA: Addison-Wesley.

Edelstein-Keshet, Leah. 1988. *Mathematical Models in Biology*. New York: Random House.

Eisen, M. 1988. *Mathematical Methods and Models in the Biological Sciences*. Englewood Cliffs, NJ: Prentice-Hall.

Erslev, A.J., and T.G. Gabuzda. 1985. *Pathophysiology of Blood*. 3rd ed. Philadelphia, PA: W.B. Saunders.

Frauenthal, J.C. 1979. *Introduction to Population Modeling*. UMAP Monograph Series. Newton, MA: Education Development Center.

Glass, L., and M.C. Mackey. 1979. Pathological conditions resulting from instabilities in physiological control systems. *Annals of the New York Academy of Sciences* 316: 214–235.

_____. 1988. *From Clocks to Chaos, The Rhythms of Life*. Princeton, NJ: Princeton University Press.

Lasota, A. 1977. Ergodic problems in biology. *Astérisque (Société Mathématique de France)* 50: 239–250.

Li, T.Y., and J.A. Yorke. 1975. Period three implies chaos. *American Mathematical Monthly* 82: 985–992.

Mackey, M.C. 1979a. Dynamic haematological disorders of stem cell origin. In *Biophysical and Biochemical Information Transfer in Recognition*, ed. J.G. Vassileva-Popova and E.V. Jensen, 373–409. New York: Plenum.

————. 1979b. Periodic auto-immune hemolytic anemia: an induced dynamical disease. *Bulletin of Mathematical Biology* 41: 829–834.

Mackey, M.C., and L. Glass. 1977. Oscillations and chaos in physiological control systems. *Science* 197: 287–289.

May, R.E. 1974. Biological populations with nonoverlapping generations: stable points, stable cycles, and chaos. *Science* 186: 645–647.

————. 1979. Bifurcations and dynamic complexity in ecological systems. *Annals of the New York Academy of Sciences* 317: 517–529.

Orr, J.S., J. Kirk, K.G. Gray, and J.R. Anderson. 1968. A study of the interdependence of red cell and bone marrow stem cell populations. *British Journal of Haematology* 15: 23–34.

Perelson, A. 1980. Chaos. In *Mathematical Models in Molecular and Cellular Biology*, ed. L.A. Segel. Cambridge, England: Cambridge University Press.

Rubinow, S.I. 1975. *Introduction to Mathematical Biology*. New York: Wiley.

Rubinow, S.I., and J.L. Lebowitz. 1975. A mathematical model of neutrophil production and control in man. *Journal of Mathematical Biology* 1: 187–225.

————. 1976. A mathematical model of the acute myeloblastic state in man. *Biophysical Journal* 16: 897–910.

Sharkovsky, A.N. 1964. Co-existence of the cycles of a continuous mapping of the line into itself. *Ukrainian Mathematics Journal* 16: 61–71.

Straffin, Philip D., Jr. 1978. Periodic points of continuous functions. *Mathematics Magazine* 51(2): 99–105.

Wheldon, T.E. 1975. Mathematical models of oscillatory blood cell populations. *Mathematical Biosciences* 24: 289–305.

Acknowledgment

The authors wish to thank Dr. Irena Sniecinski, Professor of Pathology and Director of the Blood Bank of the City of Hope, and Dr. Ennio Romano, Professor of Oncology, Pathology, and General Surgery, for their helpful discussions and advice concerning this paper.

About the Authors

William B. Gearhart obtained his Bachelor of Science in Engineering Physics from Cornell University, and his Ph.D. in Applied Mathematics, also from Cornell University. He is currently professor of mathematics at the California State University, Fullerton. His professional interests include mathematical modeling and optimization theory.

Mario Martelli received his Ph.D. from the University of Florence, Italy, in 1966 under the supervision of Professor Roberto Conti. He is currently professor of mathematics at the California State University, Fullerton. His main mathematical interests are in differential equations, fixed-point theory, and functional analysis.

UMAP

Modules in
Undergraduate
Mathematics
and its
Applications

Published in
cooperation with
the Society for
Industrial and
Applied
Mathematics, the
Mathematical
Association of
America, the
National Council of
Teachers of
Mathematics, the
American
Mathematical
Association of Two-
Year Colleges, The
Institute of
Management
Sciences, and the
American Statistical
Association.

Module 710

An Introduction to Analytic Projective Geometry and Its Applications

Kit Hanes

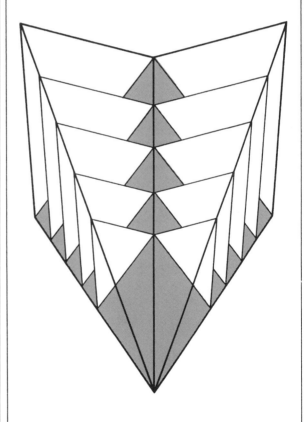

**Applications of Geometry
to Computer Graphics**

COMAP, Inc. 60 Lowell Street, Arlington, MA (617) 641-2600

INTERMODULAR DESCRIPTION SHEET	UMAP UNIT 710
TITLE:	An Introduction to Analytic Projective Geometry and Its Applications
AUTHOR:	Kit Hanes Department of Mathematics Eastern Washington University Cheney, WA 99004
MATHEMATICAL FIELD:	Geometry
APPLICATION FIELD:	Computer graphics
INTENDED AUDIENCE:	Undergraduates who have studied linear algebra

ABSTRACT: This module presents an introduction to classical projective geometry via a mostly coordinate-free analytic approach based on linear algebra. It also indicates how the theory and techniques developed may be applied to computer graphics.

PREREQUISITES: Students should be familiar with the topics in a basic linear algebra course, including eigenvalues, eigenvectors, and the Jordan canonical form.

© Copyright 1990 by COMAP, Inc. All rights reserved.

Analytic Projective Geometry and its Applications

Kit Hanes
Department of Mathematics
Eastern Washington University
Cheney, WA 99004

Table of Contents

MODULES AND MONOGRAPHS IN UNDERGRADUATE
MATHEMATICS AND ITS APPLICATIONS (UMAP) PROJECT

The goal of UMAP is to develop, through a community of users and developers, a system of instructional modules in undergraduate mathematics and its applications to be used to supplement existing courses and from which complete courses may eventually be built.

The Project was guided by a National Advisory Board of mathematicians, scientists, and educators. UMAP was funded by a grant from the National Science Foundation and is now supported by the Consortium for Mathematics and Its Applications (COMAP), Inc., a non-profit corporation engaged in research and development in mathematics education.

COMAP Staff

Paul J. Campbell	Editor
Solomon Garfunkel	Executive Director, COMAP
Laurie W. Aragon	Development Director
Philip A. McGaw	Production Manager
Roland Cheyney	Project Manager
Laurie M. Holbrook	Copy Editor
Robin Altomonte	Administrative Asst./Distribution
Dale Horn	Design Assistant

Analytic Projective Geometry and Its Applications

Kit Hanes
Department of Mathematics
Eastern Washington University
Cheney, WA 99004

1. Introduction

Projective geometry is concerned with incidence between a point and various sets of points, e.g., lines, planes or conics. It can be regarded as an extension of Euclidean geometry in which the notions of distance and angle in the latter are set aside and the special case of parallelism for lines is subsumed in an approach offering both great simplicity and generality. This classical subject includes the powerful and attractive theory of conics, which adds to its great aesthetic appeal.

Nevertheless, relatively few students meet the subject today. On one hand, it has often been presented synthetically, and the patience and discipline required for this may be a deterrent. On the other hand, when the subject is approached analytically, it is readily accessible to anyone who is familiar with basic linear algebra. Projective geometry is important for the added insight it offers into Euclidean geometry and as a step toward the study of modern algebraic geometry. At the present time, there appears to be a renewed interest in the subject, due in part to its applications to computer graphics (see Penna and Patterson [1986]).

Thus, what is presented here is a thorough introduction to some basic topics of analytic plane projective geometry, followed by a sketch of three-dimensional projective geometry. Finally, a number of examples suggest ways in which projective geometry may be of use in computer graphics.

Whenever possible, the arguments given are coordinate-free, in an attempt to make them as clean and appealing as possible.

2. Homogeneous Coordinates and the Projective Plane

Points in the real projective plane are obtained as follows. Consider the column vectors $R^3 \setminus \{(0,0,0)^\mathrm{T}\}$. Two triples in this set are defined to be equivalent provided either is a nonzero scalar multiple of the other. This relation is easily seen to be an equivalence relation, and the equivalence classes correspond to lines through the origin in R^3. Each of these classes is a point in the projective plane. Thus, a point is represented by a nonzero column triple, and any nonzero scalar multiple of that triple represents the same point. The triples are said to be a *homogeneous coordinate* system. Let $\mathscr{P}$ denote the set of points of the projective plane.

Lines in the (real) projective plane are obtained as follows. Consider the row vectors $R^3 \setminus \{(0,0,0)\}$. Again two triples are defined to be equivalent provided either is a nonzero scalar multiple of the other. Again, this is an equivalence relation, and each equivalence class is a line in the projective plane. Let $\mathscr{L}$ denote the set of lines. If $\alpha \in \mathscr{L}$, then α corresponds to a plane through the origin in R^3, the plane consisting of all vectors normal to α. That is, lines correspond to two-dimensional subspaces of R^3. A line is represented by a nonzero row triple, and any nonzero scalar multiple of that triple represents the same line.

Now let α be a line and a be a point. Let α_1 be any row triple in α and a_1 be any column triple in a. Then α and a are defined to be *incident* provided $\alpha_1 a_1 = 0$. Note that this is just the product of a 1×3 matrix with a 3×1 matrix, resulting in a scalar. It is easily seen that this notion of incidence is well-defined, i.e., it is independent of choices of α_1 in α and a_1 in a. Consequently, we commonly write $\alpha a = 0$ when α and a are incident.

The projective plane may be regarded as an extension of the euclidean plane. The idea is to embed the euclidean plane in R^3 as the plane $z = 1$. For a point p in the euclidean plane, the line through the origin and p is the equivalence class of the projective point corresponding to p. Thus, the euclidean point (a_1, a_2) corresponds to the projective point $(a_1, a_2, 1)^\mathrm{T}$. If α is a line in the euclidean plane, then the plane through the origin and α gives the projective line corresponding to α. Thus, if α is given by the equation $\alpha_1 x + \alpha_2 y + \alpha_3 = 0$, the equation of the plane through the origin and α is $\alpha_1 x + \alpha_2 y + \alpha_3 z = 0$, which corresponds to the projective line $(\alpha_1, \alpha_2, \alpha_3)$. The equation

$$(\alpha_1, \alpha_2, \alpha_3)(a_1, a_2, 1) = \alpha_1 a_1 + \alpha_2 a_2 + \alpha_3 \cdot 1 = 0$$

implies that the correspondence between points and lines of the euclidean plane and those of the projective plane preserves incidence.

Every euclidean point corresponds to some projective point. If $a_3 \neq 0$, the projective point $(a_1, a_2, a_3)^{\mathrm{T}}$, i.e., $(a_1/a_3, a_2/a_3, 1)^{\mathrm{T}}$, corresponds to the euclidean point $(a_1/a_3, a_2/a_3)$. However, for $a_1^2 + a_2^2 \neq 0$, the projective points $(a_1, a_2, 0)^{\mathrm{T}}$ do not correspond to any euclidean points. These are called *ideal* points. Similarly, every euclidean line corresponds to some projective line; and if $\alpha_1^2 + \alpha_2^2 \neq 0$, the projective line $(\alpha_1, \alpha_2, \alpha_3)$ corresponds to the euclidean line $\alpha_1 x + \alpha_2 y + \alpha_3 = 0$. However, the projective line $(0, 0, \alpha_3)$ where $\alpha_3 \neq 0$ does not correspond to any euclidean line. It is called the *ideal* line. Notice that the ideal points are all incident with the ideal line.

If $a = (a_1, a_2, a_3)^{\mathrm{T}}$ and $b = (b_1, b_2, b_3)^{\mathrm{T}}$ are distinct points, then

$$\gamma = (a \times b)^{\mathrm{T}} = \left(\begin{vmatrix} a_2 & b_2 \\ a_3 & b_3 \end{vmatrix}, \; \begin{vmatrix} a_3 & b_3 \\ a_1 & b_1 \end{vmatrix}, \; \begin{vmatrix} a_1 & b_1 \\ a_2 & b_2 \end{vmatrix} \right)$$

is the unique line incident with a and b. Similarly, if $\alpha = (\alpha_1, \alpha_2, \alpha_3)$ and $\beta = (\beta_1, \beta_2, \beta_3)$ are distinct lines, then $c = (\alpha \times \beta)^{\mathrm{T}}$ is the unique point incident with α and β.

In other words, the projective plane is an extension of the euclidean plane obtained by the addition of ideal points, all lying on an ideal line. Two distinct points (any combination of euclidean and ideal) are incident with a unique line. Two distinct lines (both euclidean or one euclidean and one ideal) are incident with a unique point. The special case of "parallel" has been removed by stepping up to the projective plane.

2.1 The Duality Principle

There are several immediate benefits from the shift to homogeneous coordinates and the projective plane. There is complete symmetry in the algebra of incidence between points and lines. Consequently, given algebraic statements leading to a theorem about points and lines, if the equations in those statements are replaced by their transposes, the result is algebraic statements leading to a theorem about lines and points. This is the basis of the

Duality Principle: If, in any true statement about points and lines, every occurrence of the term "point" is replaced by "line" and every occurrence of the term "line" is replaced by "point," the result is again a true statement.

The following theorem provides an example.

Theorem: *The three points a, b, c are collinear (incident with a common line) iff*

$$\det \begin{pmatrix} \vdots & \vdots & \vdots \\ a & b & c \\ \vdots & \vdots & \vdots \end{pmatrix} = \begin{vmatrix} \vdots & \vdots & \vdots \\ a & b & c \\ \vdots & \vdots & \vdots \end{vmatrix} = 0.$$

(The notation indicates a matrix whose columns are a, b, and c.)

Proof: a, b, c are incident with some line δ iff $\delta a = \delta b = \delta c = 0$ iff

$$\delta \begin{pmatrix} \vdots & \vdots & \vdots \\ a & b & c \\ \vdots & \vdots & \vdots \end{pmatrix} = (0,0,0)$$

iff the equation

$$\xi \begin{pmatrix} \vdots & \vdots & \vdots \\ a & b & c \\ \vdots & \vdots & \vdots \end{pmatrix} = (0,0,0)$$

has a non-trivial solution iff

$$\begin{vmatrix} \vdots & \vdots & \vdots \\ a & b & c \\ \vdots & \vdots & \vdots \end{vmatrix} = 0.$$

Taking transposes results in the following: the lines α, β, γ are incident with some point d iff $\alpha d = \beta d = \gamma d = 0$ iff

$$\begin{pmatrix} \cdots & \alpha & \cdots \\ \cdots & \beta & \cdots \\ \cdots & \gamma & \cdots \end{pmatrix} d = \begin{pmatrix} 0 \\ 0 \\ 0 \end{pmatrix}$$

iff the equation

$$\begin{pmatrix} \cdots & \alpha & \cdots \\ \cdots & \beta & \cdots \\ \cdots & \gamma & \cdots \end{pmatrix} x = \begin{pmatrix} 0 \\ 0 \\ 0 \end{pmatrix}$$

has a non-trivial solution iff

$$\begin{vmatrix} \cdots & \alpha & \cdots \\ \cdots & \beta & \cdots \\ \cdots & \gamma & \cdots \end{vmatrix} = 0.$$

Thus, the dual of original theorem states that three lines α, β, γ are concurrent (incident with a common point) iff

$$\det \begin{pmatrix} \cdots & \alpha & \cdots \\ \cdots & \beta & \cdots \\ \cdots & \gamma & \cdots \end{pmatrix} = \begin{vmatrix} \cdots & \alpha & \cdots \\ \cdots & \beta & \cdots \\ \cdots & \gamma & \cdots \end{vmatrix} = 0.$$

(Here the notation indicates a matrix whose rows are α, β, and γ.)

Other examples of the duality principle will occur below. Upon encountering a theorem, the reader should pause and formulate its dual.

Corollary: *The three points a, b, c are collinear iff they are linearly dependent. Note that if a and b are specific triples representing distinct points, then other points p on the line through a and b are given by $p = a + xb$ where $x \in R$.*

2.2 Desargues' Theorem

A second benefit is the simplification of the statements of theorems as well as their proofs. The classical Desargues' theorem is a good example.

Desargues' Theorem: *Let* a, b, c *and* a', b', c' *be two triangles such that the three lines* aa', bb', cc' *are concurrent. Then the points* $\bar{a} = bc \cap b'c'$, $\bar{b} = ac \cap a'c'$, *and* $\bar{c} = ab \cap a'b'$ *are collinear. This can be stated another way:* Suppose there is a correspondence between the vertices of one triangle and those of another such that lines connecting corresponding vertices are concurrent. Then the intersections of corresponding sides are collinear (see **Figure 1**).

Every projective theorem has its euclidean counterpart. For Desargues' theorem, it goes as follows. Suppose that there is a correspondence between the vertices of one triangle and those of another such that the lines connecting corresponding vertices are either concurrent or parallel. Then either the intersections of corresponding sides are collinear, or corresponding sides are parallel, or two corresponding sides are both parallel to the line through the points of intersection of the remaining two pairs of corresponding sides.

Just as dramatic is the contrast between the proof in the projective plane and the euclidean proof, which may need to be subdivided into as many as six cases. The various parts of the euclidean proof are subsumed by the projective proof, which we present after a lemma.

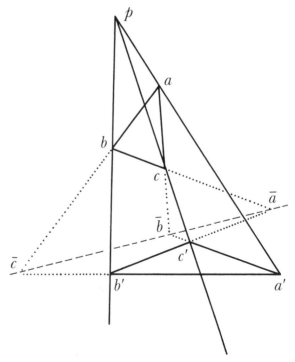

Figure 1.

Lemma: *Suppose that a, b, c are distinct collinear points. Then they may be represented by specific triples, also denoted by a, b, c, so that $c = a + b$.*

Proof: Let the points be represented by any specific triples, say $\bar{a}, \bar{b}, \bar{c}$, respectively. Since the points are collinear, these triples are linearly dependent (previous theorem), so there are scalars $x, y, z \in R$ such that $x\bar{a} + y\bar{b} + z\bar{c} = 0$. None of these scalars is zero, since the given points are distinct. Then let $a = x\bar{a}$, $b = y\bar{b}$, and $c = -z\bar{c}$ be the required triples.

Proof of Desargues' Theorem: Let the lines aa', bb', cc' be concurrent at p. It follows from the first lemma that points may be represented by specific triples, so that $p = a + a' = b + b' = c + c'$. Consider the triple $b - c = c' - b'$. Since this triple is both a linear combination of b and c and of b' and c', it represents a point both on the line bc and on the line $b'c'$. In other words, $\bar{a} = b - c = c' - b'$. Similarly, $\bar{b} = c - a = a' - c'$ and $\bar{c} = a - b = b' - a'$. Then $\bar{a} + \bar{b} + \bar{c} = b - c + c - a + a - b = 0$. Thus, $\bar{a}, \bar{b}, \bar{c}$ are collinear.

It is instructive to compare the dual of Desargues' theorem with its converse.

Lemma: *Suppose a, b, c, d are distinct points no three of which are collinear. Then they may be represented by specific triples, denoted by $\bar{a}, \bar{b}, \bar{c}, \bar{d}$, respectively, so that $\bar{d} = \bar{a} + \bar{b} + \bar{c}$.*

Proof: Exercise 1.

Suppose, as in the above lemma, that a, b, c, d are four points no three of which are collinear, and let $\bar{a}, \bar{b}, \bar{c}, \bar{d}$ be specific triples representing them, so that $\bar{a} + \bar{b} + \bar{c} = \bar{d}$. Since a, b, c are not collinear, then $\{\bar{a}, \bar{b}, \bar{c}\}$ is a linearly independent set and hence a new basis for R^3. Thus, if $p \in \mathscr{P}$ is represented by a specific triple $\bar{p}$, then there are real numbers p_1, p_2, p_3 such that $p_1\bar{a} + p_2\bar{b} + p_3\bar{c} = \bar{p}$. Relative to this new basis, $\bar{p}$ is represented by the triple $(p_1, p_2, p_3)^T$, and any other triple representing the original p is represented by a scalar multiple of $(p_1, p_2, p_3)^T$. Then relative to this new basis, $\bar{a}, \bar{b}, \bar{c}, \bar{d}$ become $(1, 0, 0)^T$, $(0, 0, 0)^T$, $(0, 0, 1)^T$, $(1, 1, 1)^T$, so a, b, c, d are represented, by these same triples or any nonzero scalar multiples of them. In other words, given four points, no three of which are collinear, they may be assumed to be the points $(1, 0, 0)^T$, $(0, 1, 0)^T$, $(0, 0, 1)^T$, $(1, 1, 1)^T$ with no loss of generality. This realization clears the way for Pappus's theorem.

2.3   Pappus's Theorem

Pappus's Theorem: *Let a, b, c be collinear, let a', b', c' be collinear, and let $\bar{a} = bc' \cap b'c$, $\bar{b} = ac' \cap a'c$, and $\bar{c} = ab' \cap a'b$. Then the points $\bar{a}, \bar{b}, \bar{c}$ are collinear (see* **Figure 2**).

Proof: In the spirit of the last paragraph, let $a, b', c, \bar{b}$ be the points $(1, 0, 0)^{\mathrm{T}}, (0, 1, 0)^{\mathrm{T}}, (0, 0, 1)^{\mathrm{T}}, (1, 1, 1)^{\mathrm{T}}$. Since b is collinear with a and c, it becomes $(\tilde{b}, 0, 1)^{\mathrm{T}}$ for some $\tilde{b} \in R$. Similarly, a' is collinear with c and $\bar{b}$, so it becomes $(1, 1, \tilde{a})^{\mathrm{T}}$, $\tilde{a} \in R$, while c' is collinear with a and $\bar{b}$, so it becomes $(\tilde{c}, 1, 1)^{\mathrm{T}}$, $\tilde{c} \in R$. Then $\bar{a}$, as the intersection of bc' and $b'c$, is found to be $(0, \tilde{b}, b - \tilde{c})^{\mathrm{T}}$. Similarly, $\bar{c}$ is $(1 - \tilde{b}\tilde{a}, 1, 0)^{\mathrm{T}}$. If $\bar{a}, \bar{b}, \bar{c}$ are to be collinear the following determinant must be zero:

$$\begin{vmatrix} 0 & 1 & 1 - \tilde{b}\tilde{a} \\ \tilde{b} & 1 & 1 \\ \tilde{b} - \tilde{c} & 1 & 0 \end{vmatrix} = \tilde{b}(1 - \tilde{a}\tilde{c}).$$

This does not look much like zero, but since a', b', c' are collinear, then

$$0 = \begin{vmatrix} 1 & 0 & \tilde{c} \\ 1 & 1 & 1 \\ \tilde{a} & 0 & 1 \end{vmatrix} = 1 - \tilde{a}\tilde{c}.$$

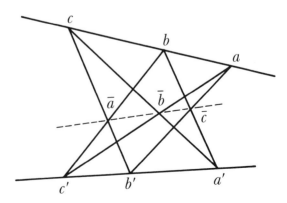

Figure 2.

These proofs of Desargues' and Pappus' theorems are worth contrasting: one is relatively clean and algebraic, while the other cluttered with coordinates but straightforward.

Exercise

2. State the dual of Pappus' theorem and construct an appropriate figure.

3. Collineations

The basic functions of projective geometry are the *collineations*, which are the bijections (maps which are both injective and surjective) from $\mathscr{P}$ to $\mathscr{P}$ which preserve collinearity. Let A be a nonsingular 3×3 matrix. Let $x \in \mathscr{P}$ and $\bar{x}$ be a triple representing x. If $r \in R$, $r \neq 0$, then since $A(r\bar{x}) = r(A\bar{x})$, the map ψ: $\mathscr{P} \to \mathscr{P}$ given by $\psi(x) = A\bar{x}$ is well-defined. Hence, we write $\psi(x) = Ax$.

3.1 Matrices Induce Collineations

Theorem: *For a nonsingular 3×3 matrix A, the map ψ: $\mathscr{P} \to \mathscr{P}$ given by $\psi(x) = Ax$ is a collineation.*

Proof: Suppose a, b, c are collinear and are represented by triples $\bar{a}, \bar{b}, \bar{c}$.
Then

$$\begin{vmatrix} \vdots & \vdots & \vdots \\ \bar{a} & \bar{b} & \bar{c} \\ \vdots & \vdots & \vdots \end{vmatrix} = 0.$$

Since

$$\det \begin{pmatrix} \vdots & \vdots & \vdots \\ A\bar{a} & A\bar{b} & A\bar{c} \\ \vdots & \vdots & \vdots \end{pmatrix} = \det \left(A \begin{pmatrix} \vdots & \vdots & \vdots \\ \bar{a} & \bar{b} & \bar{c} \\ \vdots & \vdots & \vdots \end{pmatrix} \right)$$

$$= \det A \det \begin{pmatrix} \vdots & \vdots & \vdots \\ \bar{a} & \bar{b} & \bar{c} \\ \vdots & \vdots & \vdots \end{pmatrix} = 0,$$

then $\psi(a), \psi(b), \psi(c)$ are collinear.

With respect to the underlying linear algebra, the situation is as follows. The matrix A represents a nonsingular linear transformation on R^3 with respect to the standard basis. Thus A induces a map on subspaces: one- and two-dimensional subspaces are mapped to one- and two-dimensional subspaces, i.e., projective points are mapped to points and projective lines are mapped to lines. The map preserves inclusion between subspaces, which means that incidence between a projective point and a projective line is preserved. The next theorem spells out the connection between the matrix A, the induced map on lines (two dimensional subspaces), and the row triples representing lines.

Theorem: *For a nonsingular 3×3 matrix A, the collineation ψ: $\mathscr{P} \to \mathscr{P}$ given by $\psi(x) = Ax$ induces a map, also denoted by ψ, on lines, which is given by $\psi(\xi) = \xi A^{-1}$ for each $\xi \in \mathscr{L}$.*

Proof: Exercise 3.

As with points and lines, a nonsingular matrix and any nonzero scalar multiple of it represent the same collineation:

Lemma: *Let a, b, c, d be four points no three of which are collinear. Then there is a matrix A giving a collineation ψ that maps $(1, 0, 0)^T, (0, 1, 0)^T, (0, 0, 1)^T, (1, 1, 1)^T$ to a, b, c, d. Furthermore, any other matrix with the same property must be a scalar multiple of A.*

Proof: Let $A = (a_{ij})$. Since $\psi(1, 0, 0)^T = a$, then $A(1, 0, 0)^T = xa$ for some $x \in R$, $x \neq 0$. So $(a_{11}, a_{21}, a_{31})^T = x(a_1, a_2, a_3)^T$. Similarly, $(a_{12}, a_{22}, a_{32})^T = y(b_1, b_2, b_3)^T$ and $(a_{13}, a_{23}, a_{33})^T = z(c_1, c_2, c_3)^T$, where $y \neq 0 \neq z$. Since $\psi(1, 1, 1)^T = d$, then $A(1, 1, 1)^T = ud$ where $u \neq 0$. Hence,

$$xa_1 + yb_1 + zc_1 = ud_1$$

$$xa_2 + yb_2 + zc_2 = ud_2$$

$$xa_3 + yb_3 + zc_3 = ud_3$$

Each nonzero choice for u makes this a system of equations in unknowns x, y, z which has a unique solution, since a, b, c are not collinear. If x, y, z, u satisfy this system, then none of them can be zero (e.g., if z were zero, then $xa + yb = ud$, which would imply that a, b, d are collinear, which they aren't). Each value of u yields specific values of x, y, z, and A. Any two such values for A are scalar multiples of each other and represent the same collineation.

Theorem: *Let a, b, c, d be four points, no three of which are collinear. Let a', b', c', d' also be four points, no three of which are collinear. Then there is a unique collineation mapping a, b, c, d to a', b', c', d', which arises from a particular matrix.*

Proof: By the Lemma, let ψ_B and ψ_C be collineations given by matrices B and C, respectively, mapping $(1, 0, 0)^{\mathrm{T}}$, $(0, 1, 0)^{\mathrm{T}}$, $(0, 0, 1)^{\mathrm{T}}$, $(1, 1, 1)^{\mathrm{T}}$ to a, b, c, d for ψ_B and to a', b', c', d' for ψ_C. Then it is easily checked that the collineation given by the matrix $A = CB^{-1}$ is the required collineation. The matter of uniqueness is settled below.

By now a natural question arises: are there any collineations other than those arising from matrices? The answer *no* is the content of the most important theorem in projective geometry:

3.2 ...And Vice Versa

The Fundamental Theorem of Projective Geometry: *Let ψ: $\mathscr{P} \to \mathscr{P}$ be a bijection such that $\psi(a), \psi(b), \psi(c)$ are collinear whenever a, b, c are. Then ψ arises from some nonsingular 3×3 matrix. Furthermore, this matrix is unique up to multiplication by a nonzero scalar.*

This theorem is not found in most texts, but it can be found in Artin [1957] and Garner [1981]. The proof is rather complicated. It involves showing that the difference between ψ and any collineation that arises from a matrix and agrees with ψ on four points no three of which are collinear leads to a field automorphism of the field R, and then observing that the only field automorphism of R is the identity map. Uniqueness of the matrix follows easily.

In summary, every collineation arises from a matrix and is uniquely determined by its behavior on any four points, no three of which are collinear. The collineations constitute a group isomorphic to $GL(3, R)$, the group of nonsingular real 3×3 matrices, modulo the nonzero scalar multiples of the identity.

3.3 Classifications of Collineations

Just as euclidean motions can be classified as translations, rotations, etc., so can the collineations be classified into types. The classification can be managed nicely by considering patterns of fixed points and lines. A point a is *fixed* by the collineation ψ given by $\psi(x) = Ax$ provided $\psi(a) = a$. If we drop the distinction between a point and the triples representing it, then ψ fixes a means that $Aa = \lambda a$ for some $\lambda \in R$. In other words, a is fixed provided a is an eigenvector of A. Similarly, the line α is fixed provided it is an eigenvector of A^{-1}, so that $\alpha A^{-1} = \mu \alpha$ for some $\mu \in R$.

If A is the matrix of a collineation, then none of its eigenvalues is zero, since the product of the eigenvalues equals det $A \neq 0$. Also, if λ is an eigenvalue of A, then $1/\lambda$ is an eigenvalue of A^{-1}, and the eigenvectors (in $\mathscr{P}$) for A are the same as those for A^{-1}. If λ is an eigenvalue for A yielding the fixed point a, then $1/\lambda$ is an eigenvalue for A^{-1} yielding a fixed line α.

Lemma: *Suppose* $Aa = \lambda a$ *and* $Ab = \mu b$. *Then other points on the line incident with a and b are fixed iff* $\lambda = \mu$.

Proof: Let c be on the line ab. Then $c = ra + sb$ for some r, $s \in R$. Then

$$Ac = A(ra + sb) = rAs + sAb = r\lambda a + s\mu b = \lambda(ra + (\mu/\lambda)sb)$$

$$= \lambda c$$

iff $\mu/\lambda = 1$.

Lemma: *Every collineation has at least one fixed point and one fixed line.*

Proof: Exercise 4.

Lemma: *Suppose λ and μ are distinct eigenvalues for A. Let a be a fixed point corresponding to λ and let α be a fixed line corresponding to $1/\mu$. Then a and α are incident.*

Proof: Since $Aa = \lambda a$ and $\alpha A^{-1} = (1/\mu)\alpha$, then $\alpha a = \alpha A^{-1}Aa = (\lambda/\mu)\alpha a$. But $\lambda \neq \mu$, so $\alpha a = 0$.

Lemma: *Suppose A and B are similar matrices, so $B = PAP^{-1}$ for some nonsingular matrix P. Then A and B have the same eigenvalues. If a and α are fixed by A then $b = Pa$ and $\beta = \alpha P^{-1}$ are fixed by B.*

Proof: If $Aa = \lambda a$, then $Bb = PAP^{-1}Pa = P\lambda a = \lambda b$. Hence, any eigenvalue of A is one for B, and b is fixed by B. Since $A = P^{-1}BP$, it follows that any eigenvalue for B is one for A. Likewise, if $\alpha A^{-1} = \mu \alpha$, then $\beta B^{-1} = \alpha P^{-1}(PAP^{-1})^{-1} = \alpha A^{-1}P^{-1} = \mu \alpha P^{-1} = \mu \beta$, so β is fixed.

It follows that similar matrices have the same pattern of fixed points and lines. Alternatively, the collineation arising from P above maps the points and lines fixed by A to those fixed by B. Each matrix A is similar to an especially simple matrix B, the *Jordan canonical form* for A. For nonsingular 3×3 matrices, there are just seven different Jordan canonical forms [Finkbeiner 1960]. Hence,

there are just seven types of collineations.

Type I: A has just one real eigenvalue, λ, while A^{-1} has just one real eigenvalue, λ^{-1} (the other eigenvalues are nonreal). If a is fixed for λ and α is fixed for λ^{-1}, then a and α are not incident. There is just one fixed point and one fixed line.

Exercise

5.   Prove the statement about Type I collineations. (Hint: Suppose that $\alpha a = 0$, i.e., without loss of generality, that $a = (1, 0, 0)^{\mathrm{T}}$ and $\alpha = (0, 0, 1)$, and obtain a contradiction. Then show that there can be only one fixed point and fixed line.)

Type II: A has a real eigenvalue λ of multiplicity three and the Jordan form

$$\begin{pmatrix} \lambda & 0 & 0 \\ 0 & \lambda & 0 \\ 0 & 0 & \lambda \end{pmatrix}.$$

Then $A = \lambda I$ and A gives the identity collineation. Every point and line are fixed by A.

Type III: A has a real eigenvalue λ of multiplicity three and the Jordan form

$$\begin{pmatrix} \lambda & 1 & 0 \\ 0 & \lambda & 0 \\ 0 & 0 & \lambda \end{pmatrix}.$$

Points $(a_1, a_2, a_3)^{\mathrm{T}}$ are fixed iff $a_2 = 0$. Thus, there are many fixed points, and they all lie on the line $(0, 1, 0)$. A^{-1} is equivalent to

$$\begin{pmatrix} \lambda & -1 & 0 \\ 0 & \lambda & 0 \\ 0 & 0 & \lambda \end{pmatrix},$$

and $(\alpha_1, \alpha_2, \alpha_3)$ is fixed by this matrix iff $\alpha_1 = 0$. Thus, there are

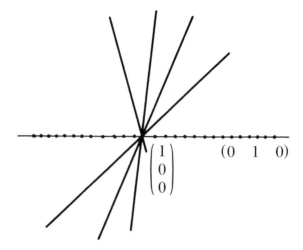

Figure 3.

many fixed lines and they are all incident with the point $(1, 0, 0)^T$. Hence, the fixed lines are all those lines incident with $(1, 0, 0)^T$; among them the line $(0, 1, 0)$ is pointwise fixed. Dually, the fixed points are all those incident with the line $(0, 1, 0)$; among them the point $(1, 0, 0)^T$ is linewise fixed. Collineations of this type are known as *elations* (see **Figure 3**).

Type IV: A has a real eigenvalue λ of multiplicity three and the Jordan form

$$\begin{pmatrix} \lambda & 1 & 0 \\ 0 & \lambda & 1 \\ 0 & 0 & \lambda \end{pmatrix}.$$

Exercise

6. Find the pattern of fixed points and lines for a Type IV collineation.

Type V: A has real eigenvalues λ of multiplicity two and μ of multiplicity one and has the Jordan form

$$\begin{pmatrix} \lambda & 0 & 0 \\ 0 & \lambda & 0 \\ 0 & 0 & \mu \end{pmatrix}.$$

The fixed points corresponding to λ include $(1, 0, 0)^T$ and $(0, 1, 0)^T$, so they consist of all the points on the line $(0, 0, 1)$. The only fixed point corresponding to μ is $(0,0,1)^{\mathrm{T}}$. A^{-1} is

$$\begin{pmatrix} \dfrac{1}{\lambda} & 0 & 0 \\ 0 & \dfrac{1}{\lambda} & 0 \\ 0 & 0 & \dfrac{1}{\mu} \end{pmatrix}.$$

The fixed lines corresponding to $1/\lambda$ include $(1,0,0)$ and $(0,1,0)$, so they consist of all the lines incident with $(0,0,1)^{\mathrm{T}}$. The only fixed line for $1/\mu$ is $(0,0,1)$. Thus, $(0,0,1)^{\mathrm{T}}$ is linewise fixed, the points on the line $(0,0,1)$ are fixed but not linewise, the line $(0,0,1)$ is pointwise fixed, and the lines through the point $(0,0,1)^{\mathrm{T}}$ are fixed but not pointwise. Collineations of this type are known as *homologies* (see **Figure 4**).

　　Type VI: A has real eigenvalues λ of multiplicity two and μ of multiplicity one and has the Jordan form

$$\begin{pmatrix} \lambda & 1 & 0 \\ 0 & \lambda & 0 \\ 0 & 0 & \mu \end{pmatrix}.$$

　　Type VII: A has distinct real eigenvalues λ, μ, ν and the Jordan form

$$\begin{pmatrix} \lambda & 0 & 0 \\ 0 & \mu & 0 \\ 0 & 0 & \nu \end{pmatrix}.$$

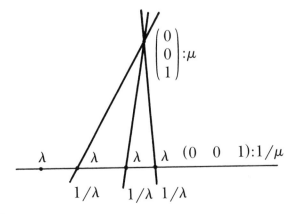

Figure 4.

Exercise

7. Find the patterns of fixed points and lines for these types of collineations.

At this point it may be interesting to consider *euclidean collineations*, that is, particular cases where the ideal line is a fixed line. For example, rotations belong to Type I, translations to Type III, and both dilations and reflections to Type V.

4. Conics

A central topic of plane projective geometry is the theory of conics, which is presented here in a way intended to emphasize the appealing interplay between the geometry and the elementary linear algebra.

4.1 Correlations and Polarities

Again, let A be a nonsingular 3×3 matrix. The map ρ from $\mathscr{P}$ to $\mathscr{L}$ and from $\mathscr{L}$ to $\mathscr{P}$ given by $\rho(a) = (Aa)^{\mathrm{T}}$ and $\rho(\alpha) = (\alpha A^{-1})^{\mathrm{T}}$ is called a *correlation*. If the square of such a map is the identity, then it is called a *polarity*.

Theorem: *Correlations preserve incidence.*

Proof: $\rho(a)\rho(\alpha) = (Aa)^{\mathrm{T}}(\alpha A^{-1})^{\mathrm{T}} = (\alpha A^{-1}Aa)^{\mathrm{T}} = \alpha a$. Thus, $\rho(a)\rho(\alpha) = 0$ iff $\alpha a = 0$.

Theorem: *The correlation ρ given by A is a polarity iff $A = A^{t}$.*

Proof: $\rho^{2}(a) = \rho(\rho(a)) = \rho((Aa)^{\mathrm{T}}) = \rho(a^{\mathrm{T}}A^{\mathrm{T}}) = (a^{\mathrm{T}}A^{\mathrm{T}}A^{-1})^{\mathrm{T}} = A^{-1\mathrm{T}}Aa$. Thus, $\rho^{2}(a) = a$ iff $A^{-1\mathrm{T}}A = rI$, $r \in R$. Then $A = rA^{\mathrm{T}}$, so $A^{\mathrm{T}} = rA^{\mathrm{T}^{\mathrm{T}}} = rA$, so $A = r^{2}A$. Hence, $r^{2} = 1$. If $r = -1$, then A must be singular. Therefore, $r = 1$ and $A = A^{\mathrm{T}}$.

Exercise

8. Referring to the above proof, show that if $r = -1$ then A must be singular.

If ρ is a polarity then $\rho(a)$ is the *polar* of a, while $\rho(\alpha)$ is the *pole* of α. Also, a is *conjugate* to b provided a lies on the polar of b, and α is *conjugate* to β provided α is incident with the pole of β. A point or a line is *self-conjugate* provided it is conjugate to itself.

Theorem: *Conjugacy is a symmetric relation. That is, if a is conjugate to b then b is conjugate to a, and dually.*

Proof: Exercise 9.

Suppose a is conjugate to b. Let $\alpha = \rho(a)$ and $\beta = \rho(b)$. Then $\beta a = 0$, and, by the last theorem, $\alpha b = 0$. Let $c = \alpha \cap \beta$ and $\gamma = \rho(c)$. Then a and b must both be incident with γ (see **Figure 5**).

Note that if the polarity ρ is given by the matrix A, then a is self-conjugate iff $a^{T}Aa = 0$, while α is self-conjugate iff $\alpha A^{-1}\alpha^{T} = 0$.

Theorem: *The point a is self-conjugate iff its polar $\alpha = \rho(a)$ is self-conjugate.*

Proof: Exercise 10.

Theorem: *No line contains more than two self-conjugate points.*

Proof: Suppose a and b are distinct self-conjugate points incident with the line γ. If p is any other point on γ, then $p = a + xb$,

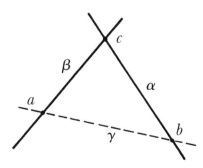

Figure 5.

where $x \in R$ and $x \neq 0$. If p is self-conjugate, then

$$0 = p^{\mathrm{T}}Ap = (a + xb)^{\mathrm{T}}A(a + xb)$$
$$= a^{\mathrm{T}}Aa + x(a^{\mathrm{T}}Ab + b^{\mathrm{T}}Aa) + x^2 b^{\mathrm{T}}Ab = 2xb^{\mathrm{T}}Aa,$$

since $a^{\mathrm{T}}Aa = 0 = b^{\mathrm{T}}Ab$. Now $x \neq 0$ since $p \neq a$, so $b^{\mathrm{T}}Aa = 0$, i.e., a and b are conjugate. Let α and β be their respective polars. Then both a and b lie simultaneously on α and β as well as γ. So $\alpha = \beta = \gamma$. Then $a^{\mathrm{T}}A = b^{\mathrm{T}}A$, which implies $a = b$, a contradiction. So p is not self-conjugate.

4.2   Tangents to Conics

Now a *conic* is just the set of self-conjugate points under some polarity together with the self-conjugate lines, which are called *tangents* to the conic. The last theorem then states that no line intersects a conic in more than two points; while its dual states that of all the lines passing through a given point, at most two of them can be tangent to a given conic. Do tangents, as introduced here, really appear to be tangent to a conic? According to the next theorem, yes.

Theorem: *A line is tangent to a conic iff it meets the conic at just one point.*

Proof: Let α be tangent to the conic given by the matrix A. Then α is self-conjugate as is its pole a, which lies on α. Thus, α meets the conic at a. Suppose it also meets the conic at another point b. Then b is self-conjugate. Since b lies on α, the polar of a, then a lies on β, the polar of b. In other words, a and b both lie on α and β, so $\alpha = \beta$. But, as before, this implies $a = b$, a contradiction. So α meets the conic in just one point.

Conversely, suppose α meets the conic at just one point, a. Let b be any other point on α. Then a is self-conjugate while b is not, i.e., $a^{\mathrm{T}}Aa = 0$ and $b^{\mathrm{T}}Ab \neq 0$. And for each point p on α, if $p = a + xb$, where $x \in R$, then $p^{\mathrm{T}}Ap = 0$ iff $x = 0$. But consider the equation

$$0 = p^{\mathrm{T}}Ap = (a + xb)^{\mathrm{T}}A(a + xb)$$
$$= a^{\mathrm{T}}Aa + x(b^{\mathrm{T}}Aa + a^{\mathrm{T}}Ab) + x^2 b^{\mathrm{T}}Ab$$
$$= x(xb^{\mathrm{T}}Ab + 2a^{\mathrm{T}}Ab).$$

In addition to the solution $x = 0$, this equation will have another solution unless $a^{\mathrm{T}}Ab = 0$. Hence, b must be conjugate to a. Thus, b lies on the polar of a. Since a also lies on the polar of a then o

must be the polar of a. Since a is self-conjugate, so is its polar α. Therefore, α is a tangent.

Suppose the point $(x, y, z)^{\mathrm{T}}$ is self-conjugate with respect to the matrix

$$A = \begin{pmatrix} a & b & d \\ b & c & e \\ d & e & f \end{pmatrix}.$$

Then

$$0 = (x, y, z) A (x, y, z)^{\mathrm{T}}$$
$$= ax^2 + 2bxy + cy^2 + 2dxz + 2eyz + fz^2.$$

If the point is taken to be in the euclidean plane, then $z = 1$, and the equation of the conic becomes the familiar

$$ax^2 + 2bxy + cy^2 + 2dx + 2ey + f = 0.$$

The tangent to the conic at the particular point $(x_0, y_0, 1)^{\mathrm{T}}$ is its polar $(x_0, y_0, 1)A$. The general point $(x, y, 1)^{\mathrm{T}}$ lies on this tangent provided

$$0 = (x_0, y_0, 1) A (x, y, 1)^{\mathrm{T}}$$
$$= (ax_0 + by_0 + d)x + (bx_0 + cy_0 + e)y + (dx_0 + ey_0 + f).$$

Thus, the equation of the tangent line is

$$ax_0 x + b(y_0 x + x_0 y) + \cdot\ cy_0 y + d(x_0 + x) + e(y_0 + y) + f = 0.$$

Let a be a point *exterior* to a conic, i.e., one through which pass two tangents to the conic, and let those two tangents be β and γ. Then the poles of those tangents, b and c, respectively, are points of the conic and are the points of tangency. Since a is conjugate to each of b and c, they must both be conjugate to a. So the polar of a is α, the line through b and c (see **Figure 6**).

Alternatively, now suppose a is *interior* to the conic, i.e., no tangents to the conic pass through a. Let β and γ be two lines through a that meet the conic, and let their poles be b and c, respectively. Again, since a is conjugate to b and c, they are conjugate to a, and the polar of a is α, the line through b and c (see **Figure 7**).

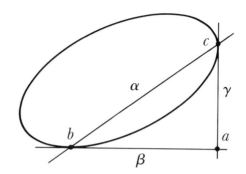

Figure 6.

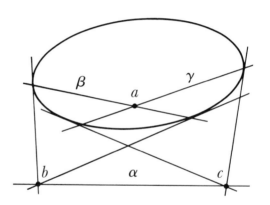

Figure 7.

4.3 Conics and Collineations

Theorem: *Collineations map conics to conics.*

Proof: Exercise 11. (Hint: You need to show that if T is the conic $\{x: x^{T}Ax = 0\}$ and ψ is a collineation given by $\psi(x) = Bx$, then $\psi(T)$ is also a conic given by some symmetric matrix.)

Theorem: *Given five points, no three of which are collinear, there is a unique conic incident with those points.*

Proof: First, suppose the points are $(1, 0, 0)^T$, $(0, 1, 0)^T$, $(0, 0, 1)^T$, $(1, 1, 1)^T$ and $(a_1, a_2, a_3)^T$. Let

$$\begin{pmatrix} u & x & y \\ x & v & z \\ y & z & w \end{pmatrix}$$

be the matrix for the conic sought. If each of these points is to be self-conjugate, then

$$u = 0, v = 0, w = 0, x + y + z = 1, \quad \text{and}$$
$$a_1 a_2 x + a_1 a_3 y + a_2 a_3 z = 0.$$

Any solution to these equations is proportional to the solution $x = a_3(a_1 - a_2)$, $y = a_2(a_3 - a_1)$, and $z = a_1(a_2 - a_3)$, and uniqueness follows from this. That the matrix obtained from this solution is nonsingular follows from the fact that no three of the five points are collinear.

Now let b, c, d, e, f be any five points, no three of which are collinear. Let ψ be the collineation sending $(1, 0, 0)^T$, $(0, 1, 0)^T$, $(0, 0, 1)^T$, $(1, 1, 1)^T$ to b, c, d, e, and let $a = \psi^{-1}(f)$. If T is the conic incident with $(1, 0, 0)^T$, $(0, 1, 0)^T$, $(0, 0, 1)^T$, $(1, 1, 1)^T$ and a, as above, then $\psi(T)$ is the conic through b, c, d, e, f. The uniqueness of $\psi(T)$ follows from the uniqueness of T.

Exercise

12. State the dual of the second theorem in this subsection.

A consequence of the last two theorems is that any conic may be mapped to any other conic by collineations *in many ways*. Therefore,

in projective geometry there is no way to classify conics as to type.

The theorems above can be used to obtain the classic theorems below. Pascal's theorem does for conics what Pappus's theorem does for lines.

4.4 Pascal's Theorem and Its Dual

Pascal's Theorem: *Let a, b, c, a', b', c' be any six points on a conic. Let $\bar{a} = bc' \cap b'c$, $\bar{b} = ac' \cap a'c$, $\bar{c} = ab' \cap a'b$. Then $\bar{a}, \bar{b}, \bar{c}$ are collinear* (*see* **Figure 8**).

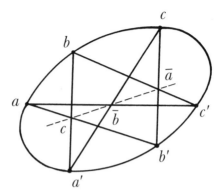

Figure 8.

Proof: In view of the theorems above, we may assume that $b = (1, 0, 0)^T$, $a' = (0, 1, 0)^T$, and $c' = (0, 0, 1)^T$. Let $a = (a_1, a_2, a_3)^T$, $b' = (b_1, b_2, b_3)^T$, and $c = (c_1, c_2, c_3)^T$. Then $\bar{a}, \bar{b}, \bar{c}$ may be found:

$$\bar{a} = c_2 b' - b_2 c = (c_2 b_1 - b_2 c_1, 0, c_2 b_3 - b_2 c_3)^T,$$

$$\bar{b} = ((a_2, -a_1, 0) \times (c_3, 0, -c_1))^T = (a_1 c_1, a_2 c_1, a_1 c_3)^T,$$

$$\bar{c} = b_3 a - a_3 b' = (b_3 a_1 - a_3 b_1, b_3 a_2 - a_3 b_2, 0)^T.$$

Now $\bar{a}, \bar{b}, \bar{c}$ are collinear provided $|\bar{a}, \bar{b}, \bar{c}| = 0$. This determinant can be computed to be equal to $-D$, where

$$D = \begin{vmatrix} a_1 a_2 & a_1 a_3 & a_2 a_3 \\ b_1 b_2 & b_1 b_3 & b_2 b_3 \\ c_1 c_2 & c_1 c_3 & c_2 c_3 \end{vmatrix},$$

which doesn't resemble zero. Since a', b, c' lie on the conic, the matrix of the conic must have the form

$$\begin{pmatrix} 0 & u & v \\ u & 0 & w \\ v & w & 0 \end{pmatrix}.$$

Since a, b', c lie on the conic, then

$$u a_1 a_2 + v a_1 a_3 + w a_2 a_3 = 0$$
$$u b_1 b_2 + v b_1 b_3 + w b_2 b_3 = 0$$
$$u c_1 c_2 + v c_1 c_3 + w c_2 c_3 = 0.$$

The determinant of the coefficient matrix of this homogeneous system is D. Hence, $D = 0$ (surprise!), and $\bar{a}, \bar{b}, \bar{c}$ are collinear.

Pascal's theorem was discovered long before the duality principle, and its dual, known as Brianchon's theorem, was discovered approximately 200 years later, about 20 years before the duality principle.

Exercises

13. State *Brianchon's theorem*. (Hint: Roughly speaking, it says that the diagonals of a hexagon circumscribed about a conic are concurrent.)

14. Prove *Seydewitz' theorem*: Let a, b, c be points on a conic, and let δ be any line conjugate to the line ab. Then the points $ac \cap \delta$ and $bc \cap \delta$ are conjugate.

4.5 Classification of Conics

All of the topics presented above may be developed independently of any connection with euclidean geometry. The latter may then be created by selecting a specific line to be the ideal line, defining two other lines to be *parallel* provided they intersect at a point on the ideal line, introducing a metric, and discarding those collineations that don't leave the ideal line fixed and that don't preserve the metric. Conics may then be classified as to type: an *ellipse* does not intersect the ideal line, a *parabola* is tangent to that line, while a *hyperbola* meets that line in two points and its *asymptotes* are simply the tangents as those two points. The *center* of a conic is merely the pole of the ideal line.

4.6 Constructing Collineations

The next proposition provides a means for constructing specific collineations of the euclidean plane. If a, b, c are ordinary euclidean points with two coordinates each, let

$$(a, b, c) = |ab| + |bc| + |ca| = \begin{vmatrix} a_1 & b_1 \\ a_2 & b_2 \end{vmatrix} + \begin{vmatrix} b_1 & c_1 \\ b_2 & c_2 \end{vmatrix} + \begin{vmatrix} c_1 & a_1 \\ c_2 & a_2 \end{vmatrix}.$$

Let $\bar{a}, \bar{b}, \bar{c}$, denote these points converted to homogeneous coordinates with 1 as the third coordinate.

Proposition: *The matrix*

$$
\begin{pmatrix}
\vdots & \vdots & \vdots \\
(b,c,d)\bar{a} & (a,d,c)\bar{b} & (a,b,d)\bar{c} \\
\vdots & \vdots & \vdots
\end{pmatrix}
$$

maps the points $(1,0,0)^{\mathrm{T}}, (0,1,0)^{\mathrm{T}}, (0,0,1)^{\mathrm{T}}, (1,1,1)^{\mathrm{T}}$ *to points* a, b, c, d, *respectively. If no three of these points are collinear, then the inverse map is given by the matrix*

$$
\begin{pmatrix}
\cdots & (a\,d\,c)(a\,b\,d)(\bar{b}x\bar{c})^{\mathrm{T}} & \cdots \\
\cdots & (b\,c\,d)(a\,b\,d)(\bar{c}x\bar{a})^{\mathrm{T}} & \cdots \\
\cdots & (a\,d\,c)(b\,c\,d)(\bar{a}x\bar{b})^{\mathrm{T}} &
\end{pmatrix}.
$$

Proof: To see that the first matrix maps $(1,1,1)^{\mathrm{T}}$ to d, consider the system of equations

$$
\begin{pmatrix}
\vdots & \vdots & \vdots \\
\bar{a} & \bar{b} & \bar{c} \\
\vdots & \vdots & \vdots
\end{pmatrix}
\begin{pmatrix} x \\ y \\ z \end{pmatrix}
=
\begin{pmatrix} \vdots \\ \bar{d} \\ \vdots \end{pmatrix}.
$$

By Cramer's rule,

$$
Dx =
\begin{vmatrix}
\vdots & \vdots & \vdots \\
\bar{d} & \bar{b} & \bar{c} \\
\vdots & \vdots & \vdots
\end{vmatrix}
= (d\,b\,c),
$$

where

$$
D = \det
\begin{pmatrix}
\vdots & \vdots & \vdots \\
\bar{a} & \bar{b} & \bar{c} \\
\vdots & \vdots & \vdots
\end{pmatrix}.
$$

It follows that the first matrix has the asserted properties. Also, it is easy to see that the product of the two matrices is just $(a,b,d)(b,c,d)(a,d,c)$ times the identity matrix.

5. Projective Three-Space

The situation in projective three-space is analagous to that in two-space. Points are represented by nonzero column vectors with four components, and two of these represent the same point, provided each is a nonzero scalar multiple of the other. The euclidean point (a_1, a_2, a_3) corresponds to the projective point $(a_1, a_2, a_3, 1)^T$. Planes are represented by nonzero row vectors with four components, and two of these represent the same plane provided each is a nonzero scalar multiple of the other. The euclidean plane $\alpha_1 x + \alpha_2 y + \alpha_3 z + \alpha_4 = 0$ corresponds to the projective plane $(\alpha_1, \alpha_2, \alpha_3, \alpha_4)$. The plane α and the point a are incident provided $\alpha a = 0$.

Points on the line incident with two distinct points a and b are represented by $xa + yb$, where $x, y \in R$. This line may be represented by the 4×2 matrix

$$\begin{pmatrix} \vdots & \vdots \\ a & b \\ \vdots & \vdots \end{pmatrix}.$$

Planes through the line incident with two distinct planes α and β are represented by $x\alpha + y\beta$, where $x, y \in R$. This line may be represented by the 2×4 matrix

$$\begin{pmatrix} \cdots & \alpha & \cdots \\ \cdots & \beta & \cdots \end{pmatrix}.$$

The line

$$\begin{pmatrix} \vdots & \vdots \\ a & b \\ \vdots & \vdots \end{pmatrix}$$

and the line

$$\begin{pmatrix} \cdots & \alpha & \cdots \\ \cdots & \beta & \cdots \end{pmatrix}$$

are the same provided

$$\begin{pmatrix} \cdots & \alpha & \cdots \\ \cdots & \beta & \cdots \end{pmatrix} \begin{pmatrix} \vdots & \vdots \\ a & b \\ \vdots & \vdots \end{pmatrix} = \begin{pmatrix} 0 & 0 \\ 0 & 0 \end{pmatrix}.$$

5.1 The Duality Principle

The *Duality Principle* in three dimensions states that if the terms *point* and *plane* are interchanged in any valid statement involving points, lines, planes, and incidence, the result is again a valid statement.

5.2 Collinearity and Incidence

Three points are collinear provided they are linearly dependent. Four points are coplanar provided they are linearly dependent. The plane incident with the three non-collinear points a, b, c is represented by $(\times(a, b, c))^{\mathrm{T}}$, where $\times(a, b, c)$ denotes the cross product of a, b, and c. It is the vector characterized by the property that

$$(\times(a, b, c))^{\mathrm{T}} d = \det \begin{pmatrix} \vdots & \vdots & \vdots & \vdots \\ a & b & c & d \\ \vdots & \vdots & \vdots & \vdots \end{pmatrix}$$

for any point d, and it is given by the formula

$$\times(a, b, c) = \left(-\begin{vmatrix} a_2 & a_3 & a_4 \\ b_2 & b_3 & b_4 \\ c_2 & c_3 & c_4 \end{vmatrix}, \begin{vmatrix} a_1 & a_3 & a_4 \\ b_1 & b_3 & b_4 \\ c_1 & c_3 & c_4 \end{vmatrix}, \right.$$

$$\left. -\begin{vmatrix} a_1 & a_2 & a_4 \\ b_1 & b_2 & b_4 \\ c_1 & c_2 & c_4 \end{vmatrix}, \begin{vmatrix} a_1 & a_2 & a_3 \\ b_1 & b_2 & b_3 \\ c_1 & c_2 & c_3 \end{vmatrix} \right).$$

Thus, the points a, b, c are collinear provided $\times(a, b, c) = 0$, and the points a, b, c, d are coplanar provided

$$\det \begin{pmatrix} \vdots & \vdots & \vdots & \vdots \\ a & b & c & d \\ \vdots & \vdots & \vdots & \vdots \end{pmatrix} = 0.$$

Proposition: *If a and b are two distinct points, the line incident with them meets the plane π at the point $(\pi b)a - (\pi a)b$.*

Proof: Exercise 15.

Let A be an $m \times n$ matrix of rank n, where $n \le m$. Then $A^{T}A$ is an $n \times n$ matrix of rank n and is invertible, so $(A^{T}A)^{-1}A^{T}$ is a left inverse for A. Suppose $p_1, \ldots, p_n$ are linearly independent points. Let

$$A = \begin{pmatrix} \vdots & & \vdots \\ p_1 & \cdots & p_n \\ \vdots & & \vdots \end{pmatrix}.$$

Then $A^{T}A$ is invertible. The following related theorem comes from linear algebra.

Theorem: *Let A be $m \times n$. Given a point q, let $\bar{q} = \Sigma c_i p_i = Ac$ where $c = (A^{T}A)^{-1}A^{T}q$. Then q lies on the line incident with p_1 and p_2 (when $n = 2$), or q lies in the plane incident with p_1, p_2, p_3 (when $n = 3$), iff $q = \bar{q}$.*

More than providing an alternative way of determining whether q lies on the line or in the plane determined by some points, this theorem furnishes a direct way of expressing q as a linear combination of those points.

5.3   Collineations

Collineations are represented by nonsingular 4×4 matrices, and two of these represent the same collineation provided each is a nonzero scalar multiple of the other. If ψ is a collineation for which $\psi(a) = Aa$, where a is any point and A is a nonsingular 4×4 matrix, then for any plane α, $\psi(\alpha) = \alpha A^{-1}$, while for arbitrary lines

$$\psi \begin{pmatrix} \vdots & \vdots \\ a & b \\ \vdots & \vdots \end{pmatrix} = A \begin{pmatrix} \vdots & \vdots \\ a & b \\ \vdots & \vdots \end{pmatrix} \quad \text{and}$$

$$\psi \begin{pmatrix} \cdots & \alpha & \cdots \\ \cdots & \beta & \cdots \end{pmatrix} = \begin{pmatrix} \cdots & \alpha & \cdots \\ \cdots & \beta & \cdots \end{pmatrix} A^{-1}.$$

Collineations may be categorized by their Jordan canonical form into 18 types. A collineation is uniquely determined by its action on five points no four of which are coplanar.

5.4 Projections

We consider projecting three-space onto a plane π from a point p not in π. Given a point x, its image under this projection is the intersection of the line through p and x with the plane π. This map sends collinear points to collinear points, so it would be a collineation except for the fact that it is not injective. As the next theorem shows, it is represented by a 4×4 matrix with rank 3. It might be called a *singular collineation*.

Theorem: *Let p be a point not in the plane π. Let ψ be the projection map that projects a point x to π from p. Then $\psi(x) = [(\pi p)I - p\pi]x$, where I is the 4×4 identity matrix.*

Proof: Since

$$\pi[(\pi p)I - p\pi]x = (\pi p)\pi I x - \pi(p\pi)x$$

$$= (\pi p)(\pi x) - (\pi p)(\pi x) = 0,$$

then $\psi(x)$ at least lies in π. In fact, the line through p and x meets π at the point

$$(\pi p)x - (\pi x)p = (\pi p)x - p(\pi x)$$

$$= (\pi p)x - (p\pi)x = [(\pi p)I - p\pi]x.$$

The ideal points comprise the *ideal plane*, which is the plane $(0,0,0,1)$. Two planes α and β are parallel provided the line in which they intersect lies in the ideal plane, i.e., provided $\times(\alpha, \beta, (0,0,0,1)) = 0$.

Example 1.

Given the circle through the points $(0,0),(0,1),(-1,1),(-1,0)$, we seek the image of this circle under the unique collineation that maps the four points to the points $(1,0),(3,0),(4,1),(2,2)$. By the first proposition, the matrix mapping the first four points to $(1,0,0)^T,(0,1,0)^T,(0,0,1)^T,(1,1,1)^T$ is

$$\begin{pmatrix} 0 & 1 & -1 \\ 1 & 1 & 0 \\ 1 & 0 & 0 \end{pmatrix},$$

and the matrix mapping these to the final four points is

$$\begin{pmatrix} 3 & -15 & 16 \\ 0 & 0 & 4 \\ 3 & -5 & 4 \end{pmatrix}.$$

Their product is

$$B = \begin{pmatrix} 1 & -12 & -3 \\ 4 & 0 & 0 \\ -1 & -2 & -3 \end{pmatrix}.$$

This maps the point $d = (-\frac{1}{2}, \frac{1}{2})$ to d':

$$d = \left(-\frac{1}{2}, \frac{1}{2}\right) \rightarrow (-1, 1, 2)^{\mathrm{T}} \rightarrow B(-1, 1, 2)^{\mathrm{T}}$$

$$= (-19, -4, -7)^{\mathrm{T}} \rightarrow d' = \left(\frac{19}{7}, \frac{4}{7}\right).$$

The equation of the circle is $2x^2 + 2y^2 + 2x - 2y = 0$, which corresponds to the matrix

$$A = \begin{pmatrix} 2 & 0 & 1 \\ 0 & 2 & -1 \\ 1 & -1 & 0 \end{pmatrix}.$$

This is mapped by the collineation to

$$A' = B^{\mathrm{T}}AB = \begin{pmatrix} 120 & -30 & -240 \\ -30 & 300 & -210 \\ -240 & -210 & 360 \end{pmatrix} \sim \begin{pmatrix} 4 & -1 & -8 \\ -1 & 10 & -7 \\ -8 & -7 & 12 \end{pmatrix}.$$

This matrix corresponds to the conic whose equation is

$$2x^2 + 5y^2 - xy - 8x - 7y + 6 = 0.$$

Its center, the pole of the line $(0, 0, 1)$, is obtained from the cross product of the first two rows of its matrix, and is

$$(87, 36, 39)^{\mathrm{T}} \rightarrow \left(\frac{87}{39}, \frac{36}{39}\right).$$

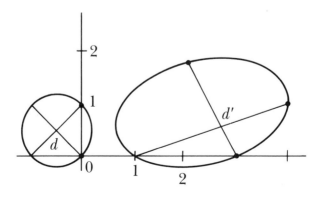

Figure 9.

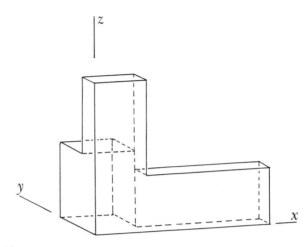

Figure 10.

As a point

$$p = \left(-\frac{1}{2} + \frac{\sqrt{2}}{2}\cos\theta, \frac{1}{2} + \frac{\sqrt{2}}{2}\sin\theta\right) \rightarrow \left(-1 + \sqrt{2}\cos\theta, 1 + \sqrt{2}\sin\theta, 2\right)^{\mathrm{T}}$$

moves around the circle, its image p' moves around the ellipse, and

$$p' = Bp = \sqrt{2}\cos\theta(1, 4, -1)^{\mathrm{T}} - 2\sqrt{2}\sin\theta(6, 0, 1)^{\mathrm{T}} - (19, 4, 7)^{\mathrm{T}}$$

(see **Figure 9**).

The remaining examples concern three views of the building depicted in **Figure 10**.

Example 2.

The building is viewed from the point $p = (-2, -6, 1)$, which is relatively close, and it is projected onto the plane $x + 3y + 4 = 0$, which is a vertical plane perpendicular to the plane through p and the near vertical edge of the building. By the last theorem, the matrix that projects onto this plane from p is

$$A = \begin{pmatrix} 14 & -6 & 0 & -8 \\ -6 & -2 & 0 & -24 \\ 1 & 3 & 16 & 4 \\ 1 & 3 & 0 & 20 \end{pmatrix}.$$

This maps the lower near corner of the building to the point $(-8, -24, 4, 20)^{\mathrm{T}} \sim (-2, -6, 1, 5)^{\mathrm{T}}$. In order to view this image, the plane π is first translated so that this point is back at the origin—this is accomplished by the matrix

$$B = \begin{pmatrix} 5 & 0 & 0 & 2 \\ 0 & 5 & 0 & 6 \\ 0 & 0 & 5 & -1 \\ 0 & 0 & 0 & 5 \end{pmatrix}$$

—then this plane is rotated so that the near vertical corner lies on the z-axis and the near right front face of the building lies in the plane $y = 0$. This is accomplished by a matrix C equivalent to a matrix of zeros in the last row and column, except for a 1 in the $(4, 4)$ spot, and the rest of which consists of a 3×3 orthogonal matrix with rows r_1, r_2, r_3. Since

$$BA(0, 0, 8, 1)^{T} \sim (0, 0, 3, 2, 5)^{T} \quad \text{and}$$

$$BA(10, 0, 0, 1)^{T} \sim (24, -8, 6, 5)^{T},$$

these conditions imply that r_1 and r_2 are both perpendicular to $(0, 0, 32)$ while r_2 is also perpendicular to $(24, -8, 6)$. Such a matrix is

$$C = \begin{pmatrix} 3 & -1 & 0 & 0 \\ 1 & 3 & 0 & 0 \\ 0 & 0 & \sqrt{10} & 0 \\ 0 & 0 & 0 & \sqrt{10} \end{pmatrix}.$$

Let $P = CBA$. Table 1 lists in its "Corners" column the transposes of the homogeneous coordinates of the corners of the building, while the column headed "Example 2]" lists the products of these vectors with P (in each case, the second coordinate is 0 and the fourth coordinate is 1, and they are omitted). The resulting projection is shown in **Figure 11**.

Table 1

Corners	Example 2	Example 3	Example 4
$(0, 0, 0, 1)$	$(0, 0)$	$(0, 0)$	$(0, 0)$
$(0, 0, 8, 1)$	$(0, 6.4)$	$(0, 4.89)$	$(0, 8)$
$(10, 0, 0, 1)$	$(5.06, 0.27)$	$(2.86, 0.47)$	$(9.49, 0.50)$
$(10, 0, 3, 1)$	$(5.06, 1.87)$	$(2.86, 0.89)$	$(9.49, 3.50)$
$(3, 0, 3, 1)$	$(1.98, 2.19)$	$(1.86, 1.22)$	$(2.85, 3.15)$
$(0, 6, 0, 1)$	$(-0.80, 0.38)$	$(-1.86, 0.15)$	$(-1.90, 0.90)$
$(0, 6, 4, 1)$	$(-0.80, 2.06)$	$(-1.86, 1.99)$	$(-1.90, 4.90)$
$(0, 2, 4, 1)$	$(-0.39, 2.65)$	$(-0.74, 2.26)$	$(-0.63, 4.30)$
$(0, 2, 8, 1)$	$(-0.39, 5.11)$	$(-0.74, 4.46)$	$(-0.63, 8.30)$
$(3, 0, 8, 1)$	$(1.98, 5.67)$	$(1.86, 2.75)$	$(2.85, 8.15)$
$(3, 2, 8, 1)$	$(1.22, 4.66)$	$(1.37, 2.64)$	$(2.22, 8.45)$
$(3, 2, 4, 1)$	$(1.22, 2.46)$	$(1.37, 1.48)$	$(2.22, 4.45)$
$(3, 6, 4, 1)$	$(0.37, 1.97)$	$(0.53, 1.40)$	$(0.95, 5.05)$
$(3, 6, 0, 1)$	$(0.37, 0.41)$	$(0.53, 0.35)$	$(0.95, 1.05)$
$(3, 2, 0, 1)$	$(1.22, 0.25)$	$(1.37, 0.32)$	$(2.22, 0.45)$
$(3, 2, 3, 1)$	$(1.22, 1.90)$	$(1.37, 1.19)$	$(2.22, 3.45)$
$(10, 2, 3, 1)$	$(3.94, 1.69)$	$(2.60, 0.89)$	$(8.86, 3.80)$
$(10, 2, 0, 1)$	$(3.94, 0.36)$	$(2.60, 0.47)$	$(8.86, 0.80)$

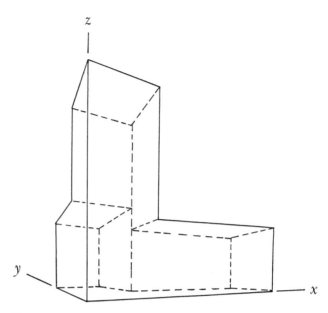

Figure 11.

Example 3.

The building is viewed from the same point $(-2, -6, 1)$ but is now projected onto the plane $6x + y + 7 = 0$. The effect is that of the eye at p gazing in the direction of the vector $(6, 1, 0)$, so that the building is seen in the left part of the image. Following the steps of the last example, the projection matrix now becomes

$$A = \begin{pmatrix} -1 & -2 & 0 & -14 \\ -36 & 5 & 0 & -42 \\ 6 & 1 & 11 & -7 \\ 6 & 1 & 0 & 18 \end{pmatrix},$$

while the matrix that translates the image of the origin back to the origin becomes

$$B = \begin{pmatrix} 18 & 0 & 0 & 14 \\ 0 & 18 & 0 & 42 \\ 0 & 0 & 18 & -7 \\ 0 & 0 & 0 & 18 \end{pmatrix}.$$

The rotation matrix that orients the image as in the last example becomes

$$C = \begin{pmatrix} 1 & -6 & 0 & 0 \\ 6 & 1 & 0 & 0 \\ 0 & 0 & \sqrt{37} & 0 \\ 0 & 0 & 0 & \sqrt{37} \end{pmatrix}.$$

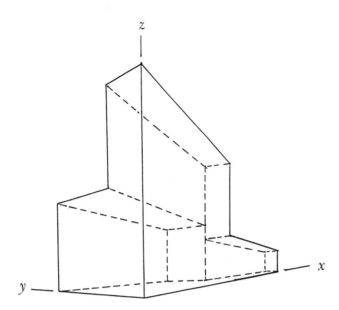

Figure 12.

Again, let $P = CBA$. The images of the corners of the building under multiplication by P are listed in the column headed "Example 3" and the resulting projection is shown in **Figure 12**.

Example 4.

Here the plane π is the same as that in **Example 2**. But the point p has moved from its location in Example 2 along a line through the origin to a location "infinitely far away." Thus, $p = (2, 6, -1, 0)^{\mathrm{T}}$. The corresponding matrices become

$$
A = \begin{pmatrix} 18 & -6 & 0 & -8 \\ -6 & 2 & 0 & -24 \\ 1 & 3 & 20 & 4 \\ 0 & 0 & 0 & 20 \end{pmatrix}, B = \begin{pmatrix} 5 & 0 & 0 & 2 \\ 0 & 5 & 0 & 6 \\ 0 & 0 & 5 & -1 \\ 0 & 0 & 0 & 5 \end{pmatrix}, \text{ and}
$$

$$
C = \begin{pmatrix} 3 & -1 & 0 & 0 \\ 1 & 3 & 0 & 0 \\ 0 & 0 & \sqrt{10} & 0 \\ 0 & 0 & 0 & \sqrt{10} \end{pmatrix},
$$

with $P = CBA$. The images of the corners are listed in the column headed "Example 4" and the projection is shown in **Figure 10**.

In **Examples 2** and **3**, horizontal lines converge to vanishing points, but vertical lines do not, since the plane π is also vertical. In **Example 4** there are no vanishing points because the observation point p is infinitely far away.

6. Solutions to the Exercises

1. If a, b, c are triples representing noncollinear points, then they are linearly independent. Thus, there are real numbers x, y, z such that $d = xa + yb + zc$. If one of these is zero, say x, then b, c, and d would be collinear. Thus, none is zero. Let $\bar{a} = xa$, $\bar{b} = yb$, and $\bar{c} = zc$.

2. Let lines α, β, γ be concurrent and lines α', β', γ' be concurrent. Let $\bar{\alpha}, \bar{\beta}, \bar{\gamma}$ be the lines joining $\beta \cap \gamma'$ and $\beta' \cap \gamma$, $\alpha \cap \gamma'$ and $\alpha' \cap \gamma$, and $\alpha \cap \beta'$ and $\alpha' \cap \beta$, respectively. The the lines $\bar{\alpha}, \bar{\beta}, \bar{\gamma}$ are concurrent.

3. Let a be a point on the line ξ. Then $\xi a = 0$. Then $\psi(\xi)\psi(a) = \xi A^{-1}Aa = \xi a = 0$. Thus, $\psi(a)$ is incident with the line ξA^{-1} for each point a on ξ.

4. If a collineation is given by a nonsingular 3×3 matrix A, then A has at least one real eigenvalue since its characteristic polynomial has degree 3, and the corresponding eigenvector is a fixed point.

5. If $a = (1, 0, 0)^T$ and $\alpha = (0, 0, 1)$ are fixed, then A must be upper triangular, so all of the eigenvalues of A would be real.

6. The Type IV collineation has $(1, 0, 0)^T$ as its only fixed point and $(0, 0, 1)$ as the only fixed line.

7. For the Type VI collineation the points $(1, 0, 0)^T$ and $(0, 0, 1)^T$ are fixed for λ and μ, respectively, while the lines $(0, 1, 0)$ and $(0, 0, 1)$ are fixed for $1/\lambda$ and $1/\mu$. For the Type VII collineation, the points $(1, 0, 0)^T$, $(0, 1, 0)^T$, and $(0, 0, 1)^T$ are fixed for λ, μ, ν, while the lines $(1, 0, 0)$, $(0, 1, 0)$, and $(0, 0, 1)$ are fixed for $1/\lambda, 1/\mu, 1/\nu$.

8. If $r = -1$ then $A = -A^T$, so $\det A = (-1)^3 \det(A^T) = -\det A$, so $\det A = 0$.

9 If a is conjugate to b, then $0 = \rho(b)a = b^T Aa$. This implies $0 = (b^T Aa)^T = a^T Ab = \rho(a)b$, so b is conjugate to a.

10. $\rho(a)A^{-1}\rho(a)^T = (Aa)^T A^{-1}(Aa) = a^T Aa$. Thus, $a^T Aa = 0$ iff $\alpha A^{-1}\alpha^T = 0$, where $\alpha = \rho(a)$.

11.
$$\psi(T) = \{y \colon y = Bx \text{ and } x^T Ax = 0\}$$
$$= \{y \colon B^{-1}y = x \text{ and } x^T Ax = 0\}$$
$$= \{y \colon (B^{-1}y)^T A(B^{-1}y) = 0\} = \{y \colon y^T Cy = 0\},$$

where $C = B^{-1^T}AB^{-1}$ and $C^T = C$.

12. Given five lines, no three of which are concurrent, there is a unique conic to which the lines are tangent.

13. Let $\alpha, \beta, \gamma, \alpha', \beta', \gamma'$ be six lines tangent to a conic. Let $\bar{\alpha}, \bar{\beta}, \bar{\gamma}$ be the lines joining $\beta \cap \gamma'$ and $\beta' \cap \gamma$, $\alpha \cap \gamma'$ and $\alpha' \cap \gamma$, and $\alpha \cap \beta'$ and $\alpha' \cap \beta$, respectively. Then $\bar{\alpha}$, $\bar{\beta}$, and $\bar{\gamma}$ are concurrent.

14. Let a, b, c be $(1, 0, 0)^T$, $(0, 1, 0)^T$, and $(0, 0, 1)^T$. Then the conic is represented by

$$A = \begin{pmatrix} 0 & u & v \\ u & 0 & w \\ v & w & 0 \end{pmatrix} \quad \text{and} \quad A^{-1} = \begin{pmatrix} -w^2 & vw & uw \\ vw & -v^2 & uv \\ uw & uv & -u^2 \end{pmatrix}.$$

If $\delta = (\delta_1, \delta_2, \delta_3)$ is conjugate to $ab = (0, 0, 1)$, then

$$w\delta_1 + v\delta_2 - u\delta_3 = 0. \tag{*}$$

Let $p = ac \cap \delta$ and $q = bc \cap \delta$. Since $ac = (0, 1, 0)$ and $bc = (1, 0, 0)$, then

$$p = \begin{pmatrix} -\delta_3 \\ 0 \\ \delta_1 \end{pmatrix} \quad \text{and} \quad q = \begin{pmatrix} 0 \\ \delta_3 \\ -\delta_2 \end{pmatrix}.$$

Then $p^T A q = \delta_3(w\delta_1 + v\delta_2 - u\delta_3) = 0$ by (*), so p and q are conjugate.

15. A point p is in the plane π if $\pi p = 0$; verify that $\pi[(\pi b)a - (\pi a)b] = 0$.

References

Artin, E. 1957. *Geometric Algebra*. New York: Interscience.

Finkbeiner, D.T. 1960. *Introduction to Matrices and Linear Transformations*. San Francisco: W.H. Freeman.

Garner, L. 1981. *An Outline of Projective Geometry*. New York: North Holland.

Pedoe, D. 1970. *A Course of Geometry for Colleges and Universities*. New York: Cambridge University Press.

Penna, M. and R. Patterson. 1986. *Projective Geometry and Its Application to Computer Graphics*. Englewood Cliffs, NJ: Prentice-Hall.

About the Author

Kit Hanes received an A.B. from the University of California—Berkeley, an M.A. from San Jose State University, an M.A.T. from Brown University, and a Ph.D. from the University of Washington, all in mathematics. His research interests lie in differential geometry and in convexity.

UMAP

Modules in
Undergraduate
Mathematics
and its
Applications

Published in
cooperation with
the Society for
Industrial and
Applied
Mathematics, the
Mathematical
Association of
America, the
National Council of
Teachers of
Mathematics, the
American
Mathematical
Association of Two-
Year Colleges, The
Institute of
Management
Sciences, and the
American Statistical
Association.

Module 713

Iterative Reconstruction in Computerized Tomography

Joanne Harris
Merzik Kamel

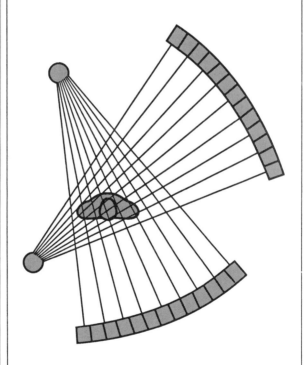

**Applications of Linear Algebra
to Physics and Medicine**

COMAP, Inc. 60 Lowell Street, Arlington, MA (617) 641-2600

INTERMODULAR DESCRIPTION SHEET:	UMAP Unit 713
TITLE:	Iterative Reconstruction in Computerized Tomography
AUTHOR:	Joanne Harris and Merzik Kamel Division of Mathematics, Engineering and Computer Science University of New Brunswick Saint John, New Brunswick, Canada E2L 4L5
MATHEMATICAL FIELD:	Linear Algebra
APPLICATION FIELD:	Physics, Medicine
TARGET AUDIENCE:	Students in a finite mathematics or a linear algebra course.
ABSTRACT:	Computerized tomography is introduced, leading to a system of linear equations. An iterative technique is presented for solving the system.
PREREQUISITES:	Knowledge of solution of linear systems. No background in physics is needed.

©Copyright 1991 by COMAP, Inc. All rights reserved.

COMAP, Inc., 60 Lowell St., Arlington, MA 02174 (617) 641–2600

Iterative Reconstruction in Computerized Tomography

Joanne Harris
Merzik Kamel
Division of Mathematics, Engineering and Computer Science
University of New Brunswick
Saint John, New Brunswick
Canada, E2L 4L5

Table of Contents

MODULES AND MONOGRAPHS IN UNDERGRADUATE
MATHEMATICS AND ITS APPLICATIONS (UMAP) PROJECT

The goal of UMAP is to develop, through a community of users and developers, a system of instructional modules in undergraduate mathematics and its applications to be used to supplement existing courses and from which complete courses may eventually be built.

The Project was guided by a National Advisory Board of mathematicians, scientists, and educators. UMAP was funded by a grant from the National Science Foundation and is now supported by the Consortium for Mathematics and Its Applications (COMAP), Inc., a non-profit corporation engaged in research and development in mathematics education.

COMAP Staff

Paul J. Campbell   Editor
Solomon Garfunkel   Executive Director, COMAP
Laurie W. Aragon   Development Director
Philip A. McGaw   Production Manager
Roland Cheyney   Project Manager
Laurie M. Holbrook   Copy Editor
Robin Altomonte   Administrative Asst./Distribution
Dale Horn   Design Assistant

1.   Introduction

Computerized tomography (CT) is an imaging technique that uses data collected by detectors when beams of X-ray photons are passed through an object. In medical applications, this object is the human body.

Imagine, for example, a cross-sectional slice, say through a person's chest, perpendicular to the main body axis. Many X-ray beams are passed through the chest in the plane of this slice, and the attenuation of the X-rays in each beam is measured and recorded. The information collected is processed by a computer, the internal features of the slice are reconstructed, and the resulting image is shown on a video monitor. (The word "tomography" comes from the Greek *tomos* meaning "slice" plus *graph* meaning "picture." CT is sometimes called *computer-assisted tomography* and abbreviated *CAT*, as in *CAT-scan*.)

In the 1970s, computerized tomography revolutionized diagnostic radiology. In the brain, for example, CT can readily detect tumors and internal bleeding without the need of exploratory surgery. The 1979 Nobel Prize in Medicine was awarded for work in computerized tomography.

The object of this Module is to consider an iterative reconstruction technique used in CT. The "solution" of a large system of linear equations is involved.

2.   Data Collection for CT

In a conventional X-ray photograph, a beam of X-ray photons passes through the body, *perpendicular to the plane to be viewed*; and the image produced is a picture of the difference in absorption of the photons by different structures in the body. The less the absorption, the greater the transmission and the darker the film. (See **Figure 1a**.)

In tomography, however, the beams of X-rays pass through the body *in the plane* of the cross-section to be viewed. In **Figure 1b**, the video monitor shows the cross-sectional slice, or reconstruction region, which is indicated by the dashed line across the body.

To collect the CT data, the X-ray source and detector positions are first translated (scanned) across the reconstruction region (see **Figure 2a**). At equally spaced stages of the translation, the detector measures and records the number of photons emerging. Then the X-ray source and detector pair are rotated through a small angle, the translation is repeated, and another set of measurements is taken and recorded. This process is repeated many times. Such a scanning mode is known as the *parallel mode*. In the first commercial scanner, developed in 1971, at the Central Research Laboratories of EMI Ltd. in England, readings were taken at 160 equally spaced positions along a single scan direction, then 160 more after each 1° rotation, for a total of $160 \times 180 = 28{,}800$ measurements.

1

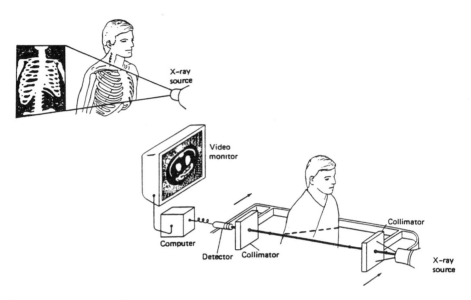

Figure 1a. Conventional X-ray imaging.   **Figure 1b.** Computerized tomography.

[Giancoli 1985, 600]

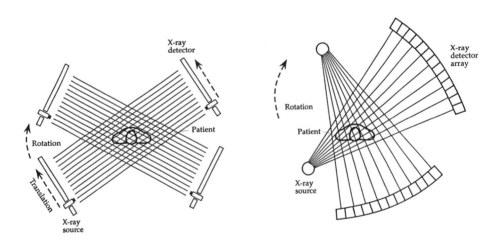

Figure 2a. Parallel mode scanning.   **Figure 2b.** Fan-beam mode scanning.

[Anton and Rorres 1991, 702]

2

Another possible mode is the *fan-beam mode*, in which a single X-ray tube generates a fan of X-ray beams and the numbers of photons emerging from the beams are measured simultaneously by the array of detectors (see **Figure 2b**). As before, the X-ray tube and detector array are rotated through many angles, measurements being taken at each angle.

The parallel scan mode requires a few minutes for the many scans needed to form an image, whereas the fan-beam mode, widely used now, requires only a few seconds.

3. CT Numbers

To reconstruct the cross-sectional image from the thousands of recorded beam measurements, the reconstruction region is subdivided into $n \times n$ small squares, called *pixels* (from "picture elements") (see **Figure 3**).

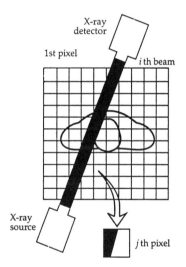

[Anton and Rorres 1991, 702]

Figure 3. Reconstruction region of $n \times n$ pixels.

The width of each pixel is chosen according to the width of the detectors and/or the width of the X-ray beams. This sets the resolution of the image, which is usually 1–2 mm. In the 1971 EMI system, 6,400 pixels were used, arranged in a square 80×80 array. The General Electric CT/T system uses 102,400 pixels in a 320×320 array. To each pixel there is associated a number, called its *CT number*, or its *X-ray density number*. This number is a measure of photon attenuation as the beam of X-ray photons passes through the pixel; it will be defined more precisely in what follows. The determination of these pixel CT numbers is the basic mathematical problem of computerized tomography.

3

Once these numbers have been determined, the cross-sectional image can be displayed on the video monitor, since from the CT number of each pixel, a "grayness" value can be assigned, and an image constructed that is made up of varying shades of gray. Different structures within the body have different X-ray densities and thus can be distinguished in the image.

It is known that, as an X-ray beam passes through an object, some of the photons of the beam are absorbed by the object (*photon attenuation*). With this in mind, consider a line of n pixels, through which an X-ray beam passes squarely (see **Figure 4**).

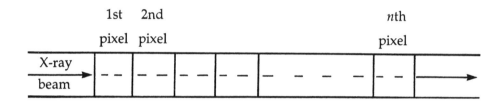

Figure 4. An X-ray passing through a line of n pixels.

Suppose that the first pixel transmits a fraction f_1 of the incident photons, the second pixel a fraction f_2 of the photons incident to it, and so on, to the nth pixel, which transmits a fraction f_n (i.e., f_i equals the number of photons entering the ith pixel divided by the number of photons leaving).

The total fraction, f, transmitted through this line of pixels will be given by

$$f = f_1 \times f_2 \times f_3 \times \cdots \times f_n.$$

Hence

$$\ln f = \ln f_1 + \ln f_2 + \ln f_3 + \cdots + \ln f_n,$$

or equivalently,

$$-\ln f = -\ln f_1 - \ln f_2 - \ln f_3 - \cdots - \ln f_n.$$

Note that $-\ln f$, $-\ln f_1$, $-\ln f_2$, $\ldots$, $-\ln f_n$ are all positive quantities since $0 < f, f_1, f_2, \ldots, f_n < 1$. The quantity $-\ln f_1$ is called the *CT number* (*X-ray density*) of the first pixel and will be denoted by μ_1. Similarly, $\mu_2 \equiv -\ln f_2$ is the CT number of the second pixel, etc., with $-\ln f$ as the total X-ray density of the beam. This last quantity is called the *ray sum* of the beam and will be denoted by s.

Then

$$s = -\ln f = -\ln(A/C),$$

where A is the number of photons that reach the detector when the target cross-section is in the reconstruction region (the actual measurement recorded for each X-ray source and detector position in Section 2 above), and C is a calibration measurement (a count of the number of photons that reach the detector when the target cross-section is not in the path of the X-ray beam). These measurements of C are taken and stored in the data collection along with the measurements of A.

Thus, if the ith beam, with ray sum s_i, passes squarely through a line of n pixels, whose pixel numbers are $j_1, j_2, \ldots, j_n$, then

$$\mu_{j_1} + \mu_{j_2} + \cdots + \mu_{j_n} = s_i, \tag{1}$$

where s_i is known from the actual and calibration measurements, and the $\mu_{j_1}, \mu_{j_2}, \ldots, \mu_{j_n}$ are to be determined.

However, not all beams of a scan pass squarely through a line of pixels. Instead, the ith beam may pass "diagonally" through the pixels in its path (see **Figure 3**). In this case, **(1)** is replaced by

$$\sum_{j=1}^{N} w_{ij} \mu_j = s_i,$$

where w_{ij} is a weighting factor that represents the contribution of the jth pixel to the ith ray sum, and $N = n^2$ (the total number of pixels).

If the beam width is the same as the pixel width, then theoretically w_{ij} equals the ratio of the area of intersection of the ith beam with the jth pixel to the area of the jth pixel. However, due to the computational difficulty of finding the area of intersection of the beam and the pixel, other definitions of w_{ij} are sometimes used. Two such definitions are:

1. $w_{ij} = \begin{cases} 1, & \text{if the } i^{\text{th}} \text{ beam passes through the centre of the } j^{\text{th}} \text{ pixel} \\ 0, & \text{otherwise.} \end{cases}$

2. w_{ij} = length of the centre line of the ith beam that lies in the jth pixel, divided by the width of the jth pixel.

The first definition of w_{ij} is easier to use than the second but is less accurate. Either of these definitions gives rise to the following system of M (total number of beams in the scan) linear equations in N (total number of pixels) unknowns:

$$w_{11}\mu_1 + w_{12}\mu_2 + \cdots w_{1N}\mu_N = s_1$$
$$w_{21}\mu_1 + w_{22}\mu_2 + \cdots w_{2N}\mu_N = s_2$$
$$\vdots \qquad \vdots \qquad\qquad\qquad (2)$$
$$w_{M1}\mu_1 + w_{M2}\mu_2 + \cdots w_{MN}\mu_N = s_M.$$

There are various methods for solving linear systems—Gaussian elimination, matrix inversion, the Gauss-Seidel method, etc. However, because of the nature of the applied problem under consideration here, which gives rise to system **(2)**, the following points must be taken into account in solving the system:

- The ray sums $s_1, s_2, \ldots, s_M$, which form the right-hand side of system **(2)**, cannot be measured exactly. There will always be experimental error in the data collected. Hence the system is usually inconsistent, and the best one can hope for is some "approximate solution." Methods of solution which assume that the system is consistent cannot, in general, be used.

- In computerized tomography, enough scans are taken in the data collection process so that system **(2)** is overdetermined, i.e., so that $M > N$. Methods of solution which assume that $M = N$, therefore, cannot be used.

- System **(2)** is so large that direct methods of solution are not feasible, due to computer requirements on storage and time.

Many mathematical approaches are being tried in the area of image reconstruction in computerized tomography. In the next section, we describe one such approach, an iterative reconstruction technique, which produces approximate solutions to the linear system.

4. Iterative Reconstruction Technique

To get the idea, let's first consider the following system of three linear equations in two unknowns:

$$1\mu_1 + 1\mu_2 = 3$$
$$1\mu_1 + 4\mu_2 = 4 \qquad (3)$$
$$3\mu_1 - 1\mu_2 = -1$$

Geometrically, this system determines three straight lines L_1, L_2, and L_3 in the $\mu_1\mu_2$-plane, as shown in **Figure 5**. These lines do not have a common intersection point, i.e., the system is inconsistent. However, points on the triangle ABC formed by the three lines can be considered as "approximate

6

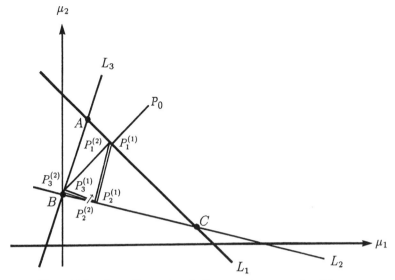

Figure 5. Iterative orthogonal projection procedure on system **(3)**.

solutions" of the system. (If the system were consistent, the triangle would shrink to a point, *the solution* of the system).

The following is an iterative procedure that generates points on the triangle ABC ("approximate solutions" of the system):

Choose an arbitrary point P_0 in the $\mu_1\mu_2$-plane. Project P_0 orthogonally onto L_1 to get the point $P_1^{(1)}$. Project $P_1^{(1)}$ orthogonally onto L_2 to get $P_2^{(1)}$. Project $P_2^{(1)}$ orthogonally onto L_3 to get $P_3^{(1)}$. The first iteration is now complete and results in the points $P_1^{(1)}$, $P_2^{(1)}$, and $P_3^{(1)}$ on lines L_1, L_2, and L_3.

Now use $P_3^{(1)}$ as the new value of P_0 and iterate again to get $P_1^{(2)}$, $P_2^{(2)}$, and $P_3^{(2)}$ on lines L_1, L_2, and L_3.

Repeat with $P_3^{(2)}$ as P_0, etc., to obtain three sequences of points:

$$P_1^{(1)},\ P_1^{(2)},\ P_1^{(3)},\ \dots \quad \text{on } L_1,$$
$$P_2^{(1)},\ P_2^{(2)},\ P_2^{(3)},\ \dots \quad \text{on } L_2,$$
$$P_3^{(1)},\ P_3^{(2)},\ P_3^{(3)},\ \dots \quad \text{on } L_3.$$

These sequences converge to points P_1^*, P_2^*, and P_3^*, say, on L_1, L_2, and L_3; and the three limiting points are independent of the starting point as long as the three lines are not all parallel [Herman 1980, 292].

We need a formula for the orthogonal projection of a point onto a line. Suppose that $Q(q_1, q_2)$ is the orthogonal projection of the point $P(p_1, p_2)$ onto the line L in the $\mu_1\mu_2$-plane described by $w_1\mu_1 + w_2\mu_2 = s$. (See **Figure 6**.)

Using vector notation and dot products with

$$\overrightarrow{\mu} = (\mu_1, \mu_2),\quad \overrightarrow{w} = (w_1, w_2),\quad \overrightarrow{p} = (p_1, p_2),\quad \text{and} \quad \overrightarrow{q} = (q_1, q_2),$$

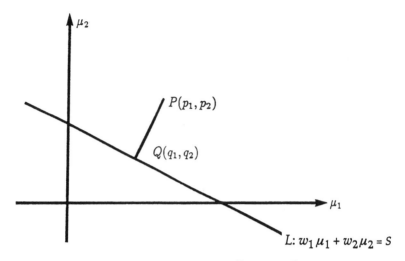

Figure 6. Orthogonal projection of point P onto line L.

then (**Exercise 1**) the projection point is given by

$$\vec{q} = \vec{p} + \left(\frac{s - \vec{w} \cdot \vec{p}}{\vec{w} \cdot \vec{w}} \right) \vec{w}. \tag{4}$$

Applying this iterative procedure to the system (3) with $P_0 = (2, 3)$ and doing four iterations gives the numerical results shown in **Table 1**.

Consider now the general case of a system of M linear equations in N unknowns, as given by (2). Instead of three straight lines in 2-space, $\mathbb{R}^2$, we now have M hyperplanes in N-space, $\mathbb{R}^N$. We will assume that these hyperplanes have no common intersection point but that we want to find "approximate solutions."

As before, we start the iterative process with a point $P_0 = (p_1, p_2, \ldots, p_N)$ in $\mathbb{R}^N$ and project it orthogonally onto the first hyperplane, to get the point $P_1^{(1)}$. This point is then projected onto the second hyperplane to get $P_2^{(1)}$, etc., resulting in the first iterate of points $P_1^{(1)}, P_2^{(1)}, \ldots, P_M^{(1)}$ on the M hyperplanes. The cycle is repeated many times, with $P_M^{(1)}$ taking the place of P_0 in the second iteration, $P_M^{(2)}$ taking the place of P_0 in the third iteration, etc.

If we set $\vec{\mu} = (\mu_1, \mu_2, \ldots, \mu_N)$ and $\vec{w_i} = (w_{i1}, w_{i2}, \ldots, w_{iN})$, $i = 1, 2, \ldots, M$, then the system can be expressed as $\vec{w_i} \cdot \vec{\mu} = s_i$, $i = 1, 2, \ldots, M$. In algorithm form, the steps of the iterative procedure are:

Table 1.

Numerical results of the iteration technique on system (3), with $P_0 = (2, 3)$.

P_0	2.0000	3.0000
$P_1^{(1)}$	1.0000	2.0000
$P_2^{(1)}$	0.7059	0.8235
$P_3^{(1)}$	0.0176	1.0529
$P_1^{(2)}$	0.9824	2.0176
$P_2^{(2)}$	0.6851	0.8287
$P_3^{(2)}$	0.0171	1.0514
$P_1^{(3)}$	0.9829	2.0171
$P_2^{(3)}$	0.6857	0.8286
$P_3^{(3)}$	0.0171	1.0514
$P_1^{(4)}$	0.9829	2.0171
$P_2^{(4)}$	0.6857	0.8286
$P_3^{(4)}$	0.0171	1.0514

1. Choose P_0, or, in vector form, $\overrightarrow{p_0}^{(1)}$.

2. Set $r = 1$, for the first iterate.

3. Compute

$$\overrightarrow{p_k}^{(r)} = \overrightarrow{p_{k-1}}^{(r)} + \left(\frac{s_k - \overrightarrow{w_k} \cdot \overrightarrow{p_{k-1}}^{(r)}}{\overrightarrow{w_k} \cdot \overrightarrow{w_k}} \right) \overrightarrow{w_k}$$

for $k = 1, 2, \ldots, M$.

4. Set $\overrightarrow{p_0}^{(1)} = \overrightarrow{p_M}^{(r)}$.

5. Increase the iterate number r by 1 and return to Step 3.

From this, M sequences of points are obtained:

$$P_1^{(1)}, P_1^{(2)}, P_1^{(3)}, \ldots \quad \text{on the first hyperplane,}$$
$$P_2^{(1)}, P_2^{(2)}, P_2^{(3)}, \ldots \quad \text{on the second hyperplane,}$$
$$\vdots$$
$$P_M^{(1)}, P_M^{(2)}, P_M^{(3)}, \ldots \quad \text{on the } M^{\text{th}} \text{ hyperplane;}$$

and it can be shown [Herman 1980, 292] that these sequences converge to points $P_1^*, P_2^*, \ldots, P_M^*$, say, on the M hyperplanes, and that the limiting points are independent of the starting point P_0, as long as the vectors $\overrightarrow{w_1}, \overrightarrow{w_2}, \ldots, \overrightarrow{w_M}$ span $\mathbb{R}^N$.

One of the points $P_1^{(r)}, P_2^{(r)}, \ldots, P_M^{(r)}$, with r sufficiently large (depending on the desired accuracy), is used as an approximate solution of the system and hence used in the cross-sectional image reconstruction. The decision of which approximate solution to use is based on different kinds of secondary criteria, which are beyond the scope of this discussion. Those interested might see, for example, Herman [1980]. A BASIC program for implementing the above algorithm is provided in the Appendix.

Even for a linear system for which $M = N$, the number of multiplications/divisions required for solution by Gaussian elimination or matrix inversion is of order N^3. The above iterative algorithm requires only a number of multiplications/divisions of order N^2 per iteration.

5.   Miniature Example

Let us consider a case for which the reconstruction region is subdivided into 2×2 pixels, whose CT numbers are denoted by μ_1, μ_2, μ_3, and μ_4. Suppose that the ray sums at four different angles are as shown at the tips of the arrows in **Figure 7**.
Then the system of equations **(2)**, with the first definition for the w_{ij}, gives rise to the following:

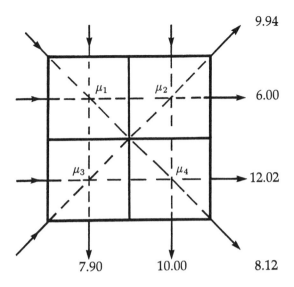

Figure 7. Miniature example.

$$\begin{aligned}
\mu_1 + \mu_2 &= 6.00 \\
\mu_3 + \mu_4 &= 12.02 \\
\mu_1 + \mu_3 &= 7.90 \\
\mu_2 + \mu_4 &= 10.00 \\
\mu_2 + \mu_3 &= 9.94 \\
\mu_1 + \mu_4 &= 8.12.
\end{aligned} \qquad (5)$$

Each of these six equations defines a hyperplane in $\mathbb{R}^4$. The convergence condition, that the $\overrightarrow{w_i}$ vectors span $\mathbb{R}^4$, is satisfied (**Exercise 2**). Using the algorithm developed in Section 4, with starting point $(0,0,0,0)$, yields the values shown in **Table 2**.

If, in the algorithm, the first definition of the w_{ij} is chosen, then the quantity $\overrightarrow{w_k} \cdot \overrightarrow{w_k}$, which is used in computing $\overrightarrow{p_k}^{(r)}$ in Step 3, is just the number of pixels through which the kth beam passes, and the quantity $s_k - \overrightarrow{w_k} \cdot \overrightarrow{p_{k-1}}^{(r)}$ is the difference between the measured total beam density of the kth ray and the calculated total beam density that would result if the individual pixel densities of the beam were given by $\overrightarrow{p_{k-1}}^{(r)}$.

That is, in the above example, using $\overrightarrow{p_0}^{(1)} = (0,0,0,0)$ as the starting point, then $\overrightarrow{p_1}^{(1)}$ (the projection of $(0,0,0,0)$ onto the first hyperplane, $\mu_1 + \mu_2 = 6.00$) is given by

Table 2.

Numerical results of the iteration technique on system **(5)**, with $P_0 = (0, 0, 0, 0)$.

	μ_1	μ_2	μ_3	μ_4
P_0	0.00	0.00	0.00	0.00
$P_1^{(1)}$	3.00	3.00	0.00	0.00
$P_2^{(1)}$	3.00	3.00	6.01	6.01
$P_3^{(1)}$	2.44	3.00	5.45	6.01
$P_4^{(1)}$	2.44	3.49	5.45	6.51
$P_5^{(1)}$	2.44	3.99	5.95	6.51
$P_6^{(1)}$	2.03	3.99	5.95	6.09
$P_1^{(2)}$	2.02	3.98	5.95	6.09
$P_2^{(2)}$	2.02	3.98	5.94	6.08
$P_3^{(2)}$	1.99	3.98	5.91	6.08
$P_4^{(2)}$	1.99	3.95	5.91	6.05
$P_5^{(2)}$	1.99	3.99	5.95	6.05
$P_6^{(2)}$	2.03	3.99	5.95	6.09
$P_1^{(3)}$	2.02	3.98	5.95	6.09
$P_2^{(3)}$	2.02	3.98	5.94	6.08
$P_3^{(3)}$	1.99	3.98	5.91	6.08
$P_4^{(3)}$	1.99	3.95	5.91	6.05
$P_5^{(3)}$	1.99	3.99	5.95	6.05
$P_6^{(3)}$	2.03	3.99	5.95	6.09

$$\overrightarrow{p_1}^{(1)} = \overrightarrow{p_0}^{(1)} + \left(\frac{6.00 - \overrightarrow{w_1} \cdot \overrightarrow{p_0}^{(1)}}{\overrightarrow{w_1} \cdot \overrightarrow{w_1}} \right) \overrightarrow{w_1}$$

$$= (0,0,0,0) + \left(\frac{6.00 - 0.00}{2} \right)(1,1,0,0).$$

The "excess" 6.00, of the measured first beam density (6.00) above the calculated first beam density (0.00), is distributed evenly between the two pixels through which the first beam passes: i.e., $\overrightarrow{p_1}^{(1)} = (3.00, 3.00, 0.00, 0.00)$, because the excess of 6.00 is distributed equally over the first two pixels. Now the first equation is exactly satisfied, by $\overrightarrow{p_1}^{(1)} = (3.00, 3.00, 0.00, 0.00)$.

In the next projection of $\overrightarrow{p_1}^{(1)}$ onto the second hyperplane, $\mu_3 + \mu_4 = 12.02$, the excess of 12.02 is distributed evenly over the third and fourth pixels, so that $\overrightarrow{p_2}^{(1)} = (3.00, 3.00, 6.01, 6.01)$ and $\overrightarrow{p_2}^{(1)}$ exactly satisfies the second equation, $\mu_3 + \mu_4 = 12.02$.

In each projection, the modified ray sum, using the projection point, is made to match the measured ray sum. However, since the rays of one projection cross the rays of another projection, each computation could partially undo the matching of the ray sums of the preceding calculations. Nevertheless, under the convergence conditions stated above, this iteration procedure will eventually give limiting values for the pixel densities.

6. Exercises

1. Verify projection formula (4) by showing that

   a) the point determined by the vector $\overrightarrow{q}$ lies on the line L, and

   b) the vector $\overrightarrow{q} - \overrightarrow{p}$ is orthogonal to L.

2. Verify that the $\overrightarrow{w}_i$ vectors of system (5) span $\mathbb{R}^4$.

3. With starting point $(1,1,1,1)$, do three iterations of the projection algorithm for system (5).

4. If the right-hand sides of system (5) were modified so that the system becomes

$$\begin{aligned} \mu_1 + \mu_2 &= 6 \\ \mu_3 + \mu_4 &= 12 \\ \mu_1 + \mu_3 &= 8 \\ \mu_2 + \mu_4 &= 10 \end{aligned}$$

13

$$\mu_2 + \mu_3 \ = 10$$
$$\mu_1 + \mu_4 \ = \ 8;$$

in other words, if we have an ideal situation with no experimental errors in the ray sums, then the system would be consistent.

a) Solve this system using Gaussian elimination.

b) Since the system has a unique solution, then the six equations must be dependent. Are the first four dependent? What about the first three, together with the fifth?

c) Do one iteration of the projection algorithm for this system, with starting point $(0,0,0,0)$.

5. Draw the three lines determined by the system

$$\mu_1 - \ \mu_2 \ = -1$$
$$\mu_1 - \ \mu_2 \ = -2$$
$$\mu_2 \ = \ 1.5.$$

Graphically perform three iterations of the projection algorithm, with starting point $(0,0)$. What will be the limiting points of the procedure?

6. A 3×3 pixel region has 12 measured ray sums as shown in **Figure 8**.

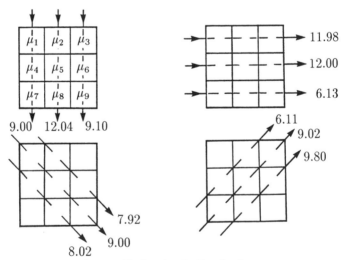

Figure 8. Pixel region for **Exercise 6**

a) Write out the system of 12 ray-sum equations.

b) Use the computer program provided in the Appendix to do seven iterations of the projection algorithm on this system with starting point $(0, 0, ...0)$.

7. Solutions to the Exercises

1. a) Since line L in vector form is $\overrightarrow{w} \cdot \overrightarrow{\mu} = s$, and since

$$\overrightarrow{w} \cdot \left[\overrightarrow{p} + \left(\frac{s - \overrightarrow{w} \cdot \overrightarrow{p}}{\overrightarrow{w} \cdot \overrightarrow{w}} \right) \overrightarrow{w} \right] = \overrightarrow{w} \cdot \overrightarrow{p} + \left(\frac{s - \overrightarrow{w} \cdot \overrightarrow{p}}{\overrightarrow{w} \cdot \overrightarrow{w}} \right) \overrightarrow{w} \cdot \overrightarrow{w} = s,$$

therefore the point determined by the vector $\overrightarrow{q}$ lies on L.

b) Since

$$\overrightarrow{q} - \overrightarrow{p} = \left(\frac{s - \overrightarrow{w} \cdot \overrightarrow{p}}{\overrightarrow{w} \cdot \overrightarrow{w}} \right) \overrightarrow{w}$$

is a vector in the direction of $\overrightarrow{w} = (w_1, w_2)$ with slope w_2/w_1, and since line L has slope $-w_1/w_2$, the vector $\overrightarrow{q} - \overrightarrow{p}$ is orthogonal to L.

2. The $\overrightarrow{w_i}$ vectors of system **(5)** are $(1,1,0,0)$, $(0,0,1,1)$, $(1,0,1,0)$, $(0,1,0,1)$, $(0,1,1,0)$, and $(1,0,0,1)$. Since the first three plus the fifth are together four independent vectors in $\mathbb{R}^4$, and hence form a basis, therefore the set of $\overrightarrow{w_i}$ vectors spans $\mathbb{R}^4$.

3. See **Table 3**.

4. a) $\mu_1 = 2$, $\mu_2 = 4$, $\mu_3 = 6$, and $\mu_4 = 6$.

b) Dependent; independent.

c) See **Table 4**.

5. See **Figure 9**. The limiting points will be $(-0.5, 1.5)$ and $(0, 1)$.

6. a)

$$\begin{aligned}
\mu_1 + \mu_4 + \mu_7 &= 9.00 \\
\mu_2 + \mu_5 + \mu_8 &= 12.04 \\
\mu_3 + \mu_6 + \mu_9 &= 9.10 \\
\mu_1 + \mu_2 + \mu_3 &= 11.98 \\
\mu_4 + \mu_5 + \mu_6 &= 12.00 \\
\mu_7 + \mu_8 + \mu_9 &= 6.13 \\
\mu_2 + \mu_6 &= 7.92 \\
\mu_1 + \mu_5 + \mu_9 &= 9.00 \\
\mu_4 + \mu_8 &= 8.02 \\
\mu_2 + \mu_4 &= 6.11 \\
\mu_3 + \mu_5 + \mu_7 &= 9.02 \\
\mu_6 + \mu_8 &= 9.80.
\end{aligned}$$

b) See **Table 5**.

15

Table 3.

Solution to **Exercise 3.**

	μ_1	μ_2	μ_3	μ_4
P_0	1.00	1.00	1.00	1.00
$P_1^{(1)}$	3.00	3.00	1.00	1.00
$P_2^{(1)}$	3.00	3.00	6.01	6.01
$P_3^{(1)}$	2.44	3.00	5.45	6.01
$P_4^{(1)}$	2.44	3.49	5.45	6.51
$P_5^{(1)}$	2.44	3.99	5.95	6.51
$P_6^{(1)}$	2.03	3.99	5.95	6.09
$P_1^{(2)}$	2.02	3.98	5.95	6.09
$P_2^{(2)}$	2.02	3.98	5.94	6.08
$P_3^{(2)}$	1.99	3.98	5.91	6.08
$P_4^{(2)}$	1.99	3.95	5.91	6.05
$P_5^{(2)}$	1.99	3.99	5.95	6.05
$P_6^{(2)}$	2.03	3.99	5.95	6.09
$P_1^{(3)}$	2.02	3.98	5.95	6.09
$P_2^{(3)}$	2.02	3.98	5.94	6.08
$P_3^{(3)}$	1.99	3.98	5.91	6.08
$P_4^{(3)}$	1.99	3.95	5.91	6.05
$P_5^{(3)}$	1.99	3.99	5.95	6.05
$P_6^{(3)}$	2.03	3.99	5.95	6.09

Table 4.

Solution to **Exercise 4c**.

	μ_1	μ_2	μ_3	μ_4
P_0	0.00	0.00	0.00	0.00
$P_1^{(1)}$	3.00	3.00	0.00	0.00
$P_2^{(1)}$	3.00	3.00	6.00	6.00
$P_3^{(1)}$	2.50	3.00	5.50	6.00
$P_4^{(1)}$	2.50	3.50	5.50	6.50
$P_5^{(1)}$	2.50	4.00	6.00	6.50
$P_6^{(1)}$	2.00	4.00	6.00	6.00

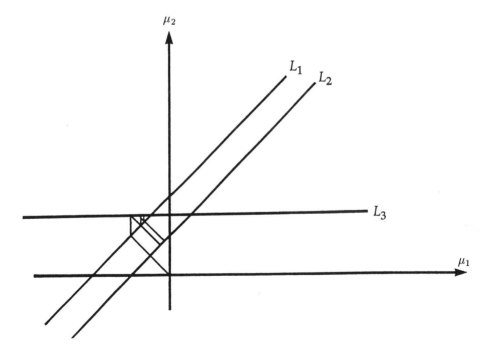

Figure 9. Solution to **Exercise 5**.

Table 5.

Solution to **Exercise 6b**.

	μ_1	μ_2	μ_3	μ_4	μ_5	μ_6	μ_7	μ_8	μ_9
P_0	0.00	0.00	0.00	0.00	0.00	0.00	0.00	0.00	0.00
$P_1^{(1)}$	3.00	0.00	0.00	3.00	0.00	0.00	3.00	0.00	0.00
$P_2^{(1)}$	3.00	4.01	0.00	3.00	4.01	0.00	3.00	4.01	0.00
$P_3^{(1)}$	3.00	4.01	3.03	3.00	4.01	3.03	3.00	4.01	3.03
$P_4^{(1)}$	3.63	4.65	3.67	3.00	4.01	3.03	3.00	4.01	3.03
$P_5^{(1)}$	3.63	4.65	3.67	3.65	4.66	3.68	3.00	4.01	3.03
$P_6^{(1)}$	3.63	4.65	3.67	3.65	4.66	3.68	1.69	2.71	1.73
$P_7^{(1)}$	3.63	4.44	3.67	3.65	4.66	3.48	1.69	2.71	1.73
$P_8^{(1)}$	3.29	4.44	3.67	3.65	4.32	3.48	1.69	2.71	1.39
$P_9^{(1)}$	3.29	4.44	3.67	4.48	4.32	3.48	1.69	3.54	1.39
$P_{10}^{(1)}$	3.29	3.04	3.67	3.08	4.32	3.48	1.69	3.54	1.39
$P_{11}^{(1)}$	3.29	3.04	3.45	3.08	4.10	3.48	1.47	3.54	1.39
$P_{12}^{(1)}$	3.29	3.04	3.45	3.08	4.10	4.87	1.47	4.93	1.39
$P_{12}^{(2)}$	4.37	3.04	3.85	3.08	3.98	4.87	1.19	4.93	0.59
$P_{12}^{(3)}$	4.69	3.03	3.96	3.08	3.99	4.87	1.07	4.93	0.30
$P_{12}^{(4)}$	4.80	3.03	4.00	3.08	3.99	4.87	1.03	4.93	0.20
$P_{12}^{(5)}$	4.83	3.03	4.01	3.08	3.99	4.87	1.02	4.93	0.16
$P_{12}^{(6)}$	4.84	3.04	4.02	3.08	3.99	4.87	1.01	4.93	0.15
$P_{12}^{(7)}$	4.85	3.04	4.02	3.07	3.99	4.87	1.01	4.93	0.15

8. Appendix: BASIC Program

```
REM IMPLEMENTATION OF ALGORITHM 2
REM EXAMPLE - SYSTEM 5
REM USING BORLAND'S TURBO BASIC (C)

REM SET THE SIZE OF THE MATRICES
REM SIZE1 IS THE NUMBER OF EQUATIONS
REM SIZE2 IS THE NUMBER OF UNKNOWNS
SIZE1 = 6
SIZE2 = 4

REM SET THE DIMENSION OF THE MATRICES
REM A IS THE COEFFICIENT MATRIX, B IS THE RIGHT
REM HAND SIDE VECTOR, AND X IS THE SOLUTION VECTOR
DIM A(SIZE1,SIZE2), B(SIZE1), X(0:SIZE1,SIZE2)

REM CLEAR THE SCREEN
CLS

REM SET THE ITERATION NUMBER (P), AND
REM THE MAXIMUM NUMBER OF ITERATIONS (PMAX)
P = 1
PMAX = 4

REM SET THE UP THE MATRICES
REM THE RIGHT HAND SIDE IS
B(1) = 6.0
B(2) = 12.02
B(3) = 7.9
B(4) = 10.0
B(5) = 9.94
B(6) = 8.12

REM THE COEFFICIENT MATRIX IS
A(1,1) = 1.0
A(1,2) = 1.0
A(2,3) = 1.0
A(2,4) = 1.0
A(3,1) = 1.0
A(3,3) = 1.0
A(4,2) = 1.0
A(4,4) = 1.0
A(5,2) = 1.0
```

```
A(5,3) = 1.0
A(6,1) = 1.0
A(6,4) = 1.0

REM DEFINE A FUNCTION TO EVALUATE THE MATRIX
REM MULTIPLICATION OF A BY X

DEF FNMMAX(A,X,K%,SIZE2)
TEMP = 0.0
FOR IDX% = 1 TO SIZE2
   TEMP = TEMP + A(K%,IDX%)*X(K%-1,IDX%)
NEXT
FNMMAX = TEMP
END DEF

REM DEFINE A FUNCTION TO EVALUATE THE MATRIX
REM MULTIPLICATION OF A BY A

DEF FNMMAA(A,K%,SIZE2)
TEMP = 0.0
FOR IDX% = 1 TO SIZE2
   TEMP = TEMP + A(K%,IDX%)*A(K%,IDX%)
NEXT
FNMMAA = TEMP
END DEF

REM DEFINE A SUBROUTINE TO EVALUATE THE ORTHOGONAL TRAJECTORIES
REM (THE TEXT GIVES FURTHER DETAILS)

SUB ORTH(A(2),K%,X(2),B,SIZE2)
   TEMP = (B-FNMMAX(A,X,K%,SIZE2))/FNMMAA(A,K%,SIZE2)
   FOR IDX% = 1 TO SIZE2
      X(K%,IDX%) = X(K%-1,IDX%) + A(K%,IDX%)*TEMP
   NEXT
END SUB

REM CHOOSE AN ARBITRARY STARTING POINT: THE ORIGIN, FOR EXAMPLE

FOR K% = 1 TO SIZE2
   X(0,K%) = 0.0
NEXT

REM PRINT THE HEADINGS
PRINT " X1";" X2";" X3";" X4"
```

```
REM PROJECT ORTHOGONALLY
REM REPEAT UNTIL PMAX IS REACHED, PRINTING OUT THE VALUES
REM OF THE RESULT MATRIX AFTER EACH ITERATION

LABEL:
   FOR K% = 1 TO SIZE1
      CALL ORTH(A(),K%,X(),B(K%),SIZE2)
      FOR IDX% = 1 TO SIZE2
         PRINT USING "##.##"; X(K%,IDX%);
      NEXT
      PRINT
   NEXT
   FOR K% = 1 TO SIZE2
      X(0,K%) = X(SIZE1,K%)
   NEXT
   PRINT
P = P + 1
IF P <> PMAX GOTO LABEL
```

References

Anton, A., and C. Rorres. 1991. *Elementary Linear Algebra—Applications Version*. 6th ed. New York: Wiley.

Brooks, R.A., and G. DiChiro. 1976. Principles of computer assisted tomography (CAT) in radiographic and radioisotopic imaging. *Physics in Medicine and Biology* 21: 689–732.

Giancoli, D.C. 1985. *Physics, Principles with Applications*. 2nd ed. Englewood Cliffs, NJ: Prentice-Hall.

Gordon, R., G. Herman, and S. Johnson. 1975. Image reconstruction from projections. *Scientific American* 233(4) (October 1975): 56–68.

Herman, G.T. 1980. *Image Reconstruction from Projections—The Fundamentals of Computerized Tomography*. New York: Academic.

Shepp, L.A., and J.B. Kruskal. 1978. Computerized tomography: the new medical X-ray technology. *American Mathematical Monthly* 85: 420–439.

Solomon, Frederick. 1980. Tomography: Three Dimensional Image Reconstruction. UMAP Modules in Undergraduate Mathematics and Its Applications: Module 318. *The UMAP Journal* 1: 102–119.

Acknowledgment

Appreciation is expressed to Michael Jory for writing and testing the computer program.

About the Authors

Joanne Harris received her B.Sc. and M.A. degrees in mathematics from the University of New Brunswick (Frericton Campus). She then accepted a position wsith the Universiyt of New Brunswick's Saint John Campus and is currently an associate professor of mathematics there. Her interests centre around the teaching of mathematics and problem solving. In 1976, she recieved an Excellence in Teaching Award from the University.

Merzik Kamel received his M.Sc. and Ph.D. in mathematics from the University of Windsor in Canada. He has taught at Mount Allison University (New Brunswick, Canada), the University of Pureto Rico, and the American University in Cairo. He is currently a professor of mathematics at the University of New Brunswick in Saint John. His main areas of interest are fluid mechanics and differential equations. He is the author of several research papers on fluid mechanics and of UMAP Module 686: Biokinetics of a Radioactive Tracer (with Joanne Harris) (*Tools for Teaching 1989*, 151–167).

COMAP's Latest Television Series Airs on PBS This Fall

AN IMPORTANT STEP IN TREATING ACID RAIN INVOLVES USING ALGEBRA. PROGRAM 7 OF *COLLEGE ALGEBRA: IN SIMPLEST TERMS* FOLLOWS THE PROCESS OF LIMING LAKES, A METHOD THAT USES QUADRATIC EQUATIONS TO DETERMINE THE CORRECT AMOUNT OF LIME NEEDED TO OFFSET THE INCREASING ACIDITY OF OUR WATERWAYS. THIS PROGRAM GRAPHICALLY DEMONSTRATES THE REAL-WORLD APPLICATIONS OF ALGEBRA.

College Algebra: In Simplest Terms, the third television course produced by COMAP, will air on PBS this fall (call your local station for details). Following the tradition of the award-winning *For All Practical Purposes* and *Against All Odds*, this introductory algebra course teaches mathematics using contemporary applications. From mail delivery to medical procedures, *In Simplest Terms* demonstrates how the application of algebra can make a delivery person more efficient, can save a consumer money, and can even spare a patient from painful surgery.

How does algebra play an integral role in measuring acid rain? What algebraic techniques are used by police when they want to determine a car's speed from its skid marks after an accident? Teaching the subject through these applications demonstrates that algebra is both practical and interesting.

A 26-half-hour television series, including text, study guide, and faculty guide, *College Algebra: In Simplest Terms* demonstrates that algebra is a language for problem solving in everyday decisions. Here television allows the teacher to expose students to a legion of possible careers, and reasons for learning algebra. *College Algebra: In Simplest Terms* gives students algebra's greatest classroom: the real world.

ORDER 1-800-LEARNER TODAY

26 Episodes, $350.

 The Annenberg/CPB Project

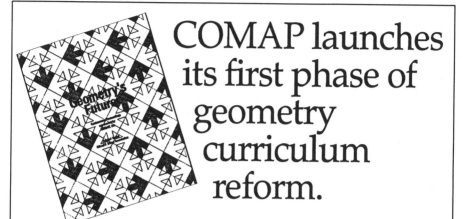

COMAP launches its first phase of geometry curriculum reform.

Geometry courses should illustrate how geometric mathematics is affecting modern life, including compact disc recorders, CAT scans, high resolution TV, image processing, robots, and map projections.

—*Geometry's Future*

Geometry's Future, a collection of conference papers that addresses the subject of geometry reform, was released by COMAP this month. The papers discuss anecdotes, actual courses, and interesting exercises that demonstrate the importance of visual thinking, and the use of geometry as a problem-solving tool. *Geometry's Future* is the first step in COMAP's plans to reform and modernize the geometry curriculum to include such subjects as motion planning for robots, symmetry and tilings, convexity, and optimization problems.

Best of all, *Geometry's Future* is available to COMAP members* for free upon request. For non-members the price is $5.99 plus $2.50 for shipping and handling.

* COMAP Membership is $32 (plus $5 for foreign membership). Write COMAP for details.

Module numbers are listed; call COMAP for a complete catalog.

UMAP Modules Applications Index

Module numbers are listed; call COMAP for a complete catalog.

Linguistics	522	617	605
215	570	652	Simulation
334	582	672	269
Living Systems	Other Mathematics	695	Social Sciences
484	87	696	84
Managerial Sciences	240	713	85
272	241	Physiology	88
509	242	251	207
626	263	341	271
649	267	Politics/Political Science	303
Marine Biology	313	296	322
607	321	297	391
Matrix Theory	323	298	406
557	335	299 & 300	428
Mechanics	425	303	429
712	461	304	476
Medicine	479	305	495
71	525	306	546
72	564	307	625
73	590	332	628
74	591	333	630
211	660	384	698
318	Photography	386	Solar Energy
377	659	394	679
456	Physical Sciences	494	Sorting Mail
686	85	495	460
709	88	620	Sports
713	211	634	579
714	546	674	683
Military Science	625	690	704
661	632	Population Growth	Statistics
Meteorology	691	345	443
658	Physics	444	487
691	81–83	587	698
Modeling	162	609	Survey Research
442	210	670	576
526	234	Practical Experience	Topology
589	292–293	538	216
Modular Systems	324	578	231
567	325	629	Utility Theory
Music	331	641	394
588	341	Probability	Visual Perception
Navigation	427	520	534
597	431	614	Voting Theory
Nutrition	468	694	535
684	473	Psychology	690
Oceanography	490	251	Winemaking
292–293	497	534	705
Operations Research	507	535	
107 & 111	517	539	
272	554	Rational Choice	
340	600	394	
453	601	Scheduling	
454	602	657	
687	603	Sciences	
Optimization	609	86	

Module numbers are listed; call COMAP for a complete catalog.

UMAP Modules Mathematical Topic Index

Abstract Algebra
310
460
461
476
557

Algebra
321
366
381
673
688

Algorithms
477
478

Analysis
318
324
325
326
334
427
468
490
522
530
592
609
708

Analytic Geometry
565

Applied Finite
Mathematics
528

Applied
Mathematics
681

Business
Mathematics
685

Calculus
60–62
67
68
69
70
71
72
73
74
75
86
87
88
162
203–205
206
210
211
215
216
232
234
240
241
242
251
270
294
296
299–300
321
323
331
334
341
379
382
396
425
426
431
432
444
473
494
502
506

507
508
517
518
525
553
554
565
566
570
611
614
625
635
638
640
661
670
674
678
679
686
693
694
696
702
705
708
712
714
716

Computer Science
263
264

Derivatives of
Trigonometric
Function
158–161

Differential
Calculus
376

Differential
Equations
81–83

303
308
322
335
484
497
534
535
610
617
628
632
653
670
676
686
695
696
702

Discrete
Mathematics
105 & 109
106 & 110
107 & 111
108 & 112
269
272
297
298
304
305
306
307
317
332
333
334
381
384
386
390
394
395
442
453
454
476
495

Module numbers are listed; call COMAP for a complete catalog.

520
568
571
582
589
591
605
620
657
671
687
690
692
709

Elementary Analytic Geometry
635

Elementary Functions
84
85

Game Theory
311

Geometry
231
267
479
594
597
660
710

Linear Algebra
207
208
209
313
336
337
339
345
346
526
558

569
649
652
684
704

Linear Programming
687

Mathematical Modeling
690

Matrix Multiplication
672

Number Theory
633

Precalculus Mathematics
292–293
297
298
304
305
306
307
332
333
334
367–369
370–372
373–374
375
474
479
511
539
546
551
560
562
564
567
577

578
580
584
588
600
601
602
603
607
639
641
658
659
662
668
675
677
678
689
691

Probability and Statistics
268
271
327
330
340
377
391
406
428
429
433
443
456
487
533
538
555
572
574
576
579
587
590
612
614
626

629
630
631
634
649
651
683
698
699